Photographic I

1. Portrait of Maria Anna Mozart,

2. Maria Anna Mozart as a child, 1763. Portrait said to be by Pietro Antonio Lorenzoni.

3. The Boy Mozart. Anonymous portrait of the child Mozart, 1763, possibly also by Pietro Antonio Lorenzoni.

4. Wolfgang Amadeus Mozart, 1780, by Johann Nepomuk della Croce.

5. Leopold Mozart and his children, Wolfgang and Maria Anna, on tour. Watercolour by Carmontelle, 1763.

6. Portrait of Fanny Hensel, 1842. Oil on canvas by Moritz Daniel Oppenheim.

7. Fanny Mendelssohn sketched by her future husband, Wilhelm Hensel.

8. Portrait of Felix Mendelssohn by the English Miniaturist James Warren Childe. Watercolour, 1839.

9. Clara Wieck from a lithograph, 1835.

10. Clara Schumann.

11. Robert Schumann, lithograph by Josef Kriehuber, 1839.

12. Photograph of Nadezhda Nikolayevna Rimskaya- Korsakova née Purgold.

MUSICAL RELATIONS

by

Angela Bradley

Bright Pen

A Bright Pen Book

Text Copyright © Angela Bradley 2011

Cover design by Angela Bradley ©

British Library Cataloguing Publication Data.
A catalogue record for this book is available from the British Library

ISBN 978-07552-1344-3

Authors OnLine Ltd
19 The Cinques
Gamlingay, Sandy
Bedfordshire SG19 3NU
England

This book is also available in e-book format, details of which are available at www.authorsonline.co.uk

Acknowledgements

Adriano of Zurich for the photograph of Ottorino and Elsa Respighi in the garden of their Rome villa I Pini, 1933.

The Royal College of Music, London, for Jessie and the children and Samuel Coleridge Taylor and family.

The Britten-Pears Foundation for the photograph of Gustav Holst, 1923 and of Imogen Holst conducting at Dartington 1942.

Contents

Introduction

"I once thought I possessed creative talent, but I have given up this idea; a woman must not desire to compose – there has never yet been one able to, and why should I expect to be the one?"

Clara Schumann wrote this sad observation in her diary, in 1839.

She had composed music from childhood and been acknowledged as a brilliant pianist. At the age of nine she had made her debut, and continued to perform in concert halls in many towns and cities, but on reaching 20 she had realised that, as an adult, this role would no longer be open to her. The child prodigy, now grown to womanhood must conform and live her life as was deemed proper for women, at that time.

Clara Schumann is one of eight female performers and composers featured in this book, from Maria Mozart born in 1751 to Imogen Holst who died in 1984.

It is not only because of their musical prowess and desire to compose that I have selected these eight women, but because of their relationship with a famous male composer. As a sister, wife or daughter it is my aim to discuss whether this was an asset or not to their own musical careers, and to show how the times in which they lived affected their freedom to follow their own talents and musical interests.

There have been a considerable number of female composers over the centuries but only a few are generally well known. Many were successful during their lifetime but forgotten after their death.

This is based on centuries of male bias. Men had careers as musicians and composers, women merely dabbled, when they had time, and were therefore not taken seriously. It was considered that the brains of women were inferior and lacked the capacity for creativity. Men wielded the power and women accepted it. It was even considered dangerous for women to acquire knowledge, as it might have deflected from their role as a good wife, housekeeper and mother.

In the 18th and 19th centuries lack of education for women had become the greatest obstacle. Some were fortunate to be born into a musical family, able to grow up with music all around them. Fanny Mendelssohn, for example, shared the same musical tuition as her brother, Felix, and yet social attitudes, voiced by her father, completely discouraged her hopes for the future;

" --- for Felix music will become a profession, while for you it will always remain but an ornament."

As women were unable to take up any musical positions, professionally, their chief outlet was centred around accomplishments permitted at home. Playing a keyboard instrument fitted comfortably into this domestic setting, and in this way women were encouraged to play and sing as an entertainment for parties and social gatherings. Many composed songs and chamber music for this purpose but these compositions remained mainly unpublished and shunned by experts. The female status implied being an amateur.

This, therefore, was the situation that Maria Anna Mozart, Fanny Mendelssohn and Clara Schumann, had, unfortunately, to accept, even though they had all proved to possess exceptional musical talent. Clara had been born into a musical family but married a composer. Maria and Fanny's relationships were as sister to a famous brother.

Nadezhda Rimsky- Korsakov, Alma Mahler, and Elsa Respighi, born in the second half of the 19th century, became wives of famous composers and their roles were more as promoters of their husbands' work rather than as performers themselves.

It is with Avril Coleridge Taylor and Imogen Holst, both

daughters of famous composers, that we see how much freedom and encouragement was given to women in the 20th century as opposed to the 18th and 19th. They both grew up in a musical world, even though Avril's father, Samuel, died when she was only nine, and both were encouraged to lead a life of fulfilment as professional musicians.

Now that women are more readily accepted as composers, compositions, by those long forgotten, are being searched for and recorded, but there is still, a long way to go.

The BBC annual Promenade Concerts, recognised as the greatest music festival in the world, spanning eight weeks every summer, rarely feature compositions by women. At best the programme has contained work by five women as opposed to that of 60 or more men.

In 1996 there was only one work by a woman, a piano trio by Clara Schumann, selected to celebrate the 100th anniversary of her death.

She had outlived her husband, Robert, by 40 years and following his death, was forced to be the breadwinner for her large family, by playing in concerts, and teaching. Her own compositions were not sought after. She gave up composing at the age of 36.

How delighted she would have been to know that, at last, her works are being recognised and performed.

Quoted from her diary in 1846:

"There is nothing greater than the joy of composing something oneself and then listening to it."

1. A portrait of Maria Anna Mozart, ca. 1785

2. Maria Anna Mozart as a child (1763) – portrait said to be by Lorenzoni.

3. Anonymous portrait of the child Mozart, possibly by Pietro Antonio Lorenzoni; painted in 1763 on commission from Leopold

4. Mozart circa 1780, by Johann Nepomuk della Croce

5. The Mozart family on tour:
Leopold, Wolfgang, and Nannerl.
Watercolor by Carmontelle, ca. 1763

Chapter One

Maria "Nannerl" Mozart.

1751 - 1829

"Mademoiselle Mozart, now thirteen years of age, and moreover grown much prettier, has the most beautiful and most brilliant execution on the harpsichord ---- her brother alone is capable of robbing her of supremacy."

This comment was made by Baron Grimm, critic and author of *Correspondance Littéraire,* who, with his mistress, Madame d'Epinay, befriended the Mozart family when they arrived in Paris, in November 1763.

They had been touring since July, the two children performing to delighted audiences, but it was becoming obvious to Nannerl that her adored brother, Wolfgang, who was five years her junior, was showing such remarkable musical prowess that she, although talented and hard working herself, was finding it hard to keep up.

It might be considered that Nannerl was, in fact, lucky to have survived infancy, the only one out of six children to do so, until her mother, Anna Maria, with great difficulty, gave birth to her seventh and last child, Johann Chrysostomus Wolfgang Theophilus.

Anna Maria's first three children had been born within two years of her marriage and they had all died a few months after their birth. In the summer of 1750 she had begged to go for a health cure at Bad Gastein, which, although using precious money, had proved very beneficial. Nannerl, christened Maria Anna Walburga Ignatia, was born on 31st July 1751, and although suffering many serious illnesses, survived into her 79th year, outliving her less robust brother, Wolfgang, by 38 years.

Leopold, their father had become increasingly impatient with Anna Maria's constant childbearing and the domestic turbulence that it caused, forcing him to take time away from his work that, at the time of Wolfgang's birth, was a book on the fundamental principles of playing the violin. To his publisher, Johann Lotter, he wrote,

"I can assure you I have so much to do that I sometimes don't know where my head is - when the wife is in childbed there is always someone turning up to rob you of time."

However, his priorities soon changed when he realised that his two surviving children possessed an abundance of musical talent.

Music, as a means of earning a living, featured on both sides of the family. The father of their maternal grandmother, Eva Rosina, and her first husband, had been church musicians in Saltzburg.

Her second husband, Nikolaus Pertl, Anna Maria's father, a graduate in law from the Benedictine University in Saltzburg, sung bass in the choir of St. Peter's Abbey. He was 45 when he married Eva Rosina and held a senior post as District Superintendent in St. Andrae. However in 1715 he suffered a debilitating illness, was unable to work, and fell badly in debt. He died in March 1724.

Anna Maria was, at that time, only four, her sister, Maria Rosina, just a year older. After their father's death they moved from St. Gilgen to Saltzburg where Eva Rosina and her two daughters survived on a charity pension. Their life was one of poverty. Maria Rosina died at the age of nine and Anna Maria was constantly ill. Her education was limited, but she developed a strong sense of duty and loyalty as she grew to adulthood, in caring for her widowed mother.

In 1747 she married Leopold Mozart. They rented a small apartment on Getreidegasse, and moved in, together with Eva

Rosina, who was to live with them for the duration of her lifetime. This apartment was home to the family for 26 years. The owner was a prosperous merchant, Johann Lorenz Hagenauer. He became a lifelong friend of the Mozart family and assisted Leopold with financial contacts whilst travelling abroad.

Leopold began his musical career as a choirboy and he became a skilled violinist, organist and teacher. His parents wanted him to be a Catholic priest but, defying them, he opted to enrol at the Benedictine University in Saltzsburg and was awarded a degree of Bachelor of Philosophy in 1738. In 1740 he began a career as a professional musician, eventually becoming deputy Kapellmeister to the Court Orchestra of the Archbishop of Saltzburg.

This was his ultimate position and it is probable that he rose no further primarily because of his devotion to the talents of his children, especially Wolfgang, and because he was constantly absent from Court due to the lengthy tours on which he took them.

Like their mother, the two children received no formal education but were tutored by their father at home. He was a very caring and competent teacher. Both the children wrote clearly, read and drew well and were articulate in speech. Leopold also taught them history, geography, arithmetic and music in which they showed natural interest and enthusiasm. They had been surrounded by it from an early age, when fellow Court musicians visited the apartment to play and rehearse.

Nannerl was seven years old when her father began to give her keyboard lessons on the clavier, and she seemed, to him, to be a potential child prodigy. These few years before her brother's amazing talents emerged must have endeared her to her father, and he compiled a book of short pieces for her, by himself and other composers, arranged in order of difficulty and entitled, *Ce livre appartient á Marie Anna Mozart, 1759.*

It wasn't long before the three-year old Mozart began to pick out some of these tunes on the keyboard, causing Nannerl to write in her diary, *"in the fourth year of his age his father began to teach him minuets and pieces at the clavier. ---- he could play faultlessly – keeping exactly in time."*

Later she recorded, "*at the age of five he was already composing little pieces, which he played to his father who wrote them down.*"

To Leopold the discovery that his son appeared to possess an astonishing musical talent at such an early age was a life changing experience. He is known to have referred to Wolfgang as "*the miracle that God let be born in Saltzburg,*" and from making this discovery he re-organised his life in order to promote the genius of his children, especially Wolfgang, to the world.

Thus began the series of tours.

In the winter of 1762 when Nannerl was ten and Wolfgang, six, they travelled to Munich to play for the Elector Maximilian III. The experience was a great success and thus encouraged, Leopold arranged another tour for the following September, to Vienna.

The children were seen and heard everywhere, including the palace of Schonnbrunn where they played before the Empress Maria Theresa. They were befriended by the young Archdukes and Archduchesses, and given fashionable clothes by them in which they had their portraits painted.

Unfortunately Wolfgang became ill, an occurrence that constantly plagued him all his life. Generally speaking, though, the tour was considered a huge success, one week's payment amounting to more than Leopold earned in two years, in Saltzburg.

Count Zinzendorf, a councillor at the Treasury wrote of the children, in his diary,

"*The poor, little fellow plays marvellously, he is a child of spirit, lively, charming; -- his sister's playing is masterly.*"

Even at this early stage it was evident that Wolfgang was beginning to overshadow Nannerl especially as he was the younger of the two and performed his own compositions. But even so this sister - brother act was sensational and as siblings their closeness was maximised in the make believe world that they created together called *The Kingdom of Back* where Wolfgang was King and Nannerl Queen. Their fantasies were played out inspired by the experience of travelling around the Courts of Europe.

The longest tour lasted for three and a half years from June 1763 to November 1766 and included visits to Munich, Paris and

London. Everywhere they stayed they performed and were well rewarded.

Leopold summarised this success in one of his letters to Johann Hagenauer,

"What it all amounts to is this, that my little girl, although she is only twelve years old, is one of the most skilful players in Europe, and that, in a word, my boy knows in his eighth year what one would expect only from a man of forty."

This tour was the highlight of Nannerl's young life and years later she could remember every detail especially the exciting Christmas spent in Paris and the visit to Versailles. Then there was the challenge of learning different languages, the joy of attending ballets and operas and the pleasure of seeing the beauty of art in paintings and architecture - a fine education indeed.

In April 1764 their destination was London. The fascination of sea travel, for the first time was overshadowed by horrible seasickness as they crossed the Channel to Dover. However, again, this venture began successfully, and they remained in England for 15 months, played for King George III and Queen Charlotte twice, for which they received 24 guineas each time. They met musicians such as Johann Christian Bach, son of Johann Sebastian, listened to a diversity of music and received a gratifying amount of money and gifts.

This success, however, was interrupted by Leopold's long summer illness. The family decided to move to the country where Anna Maria nursed her husband and looked after the family. To while away the time Wolfgang began to compose symphonies that Nannerl carefully wrote down for him.

After his recovery, Leopold attempted to recreate interest in his children's prowess but having little success the family sailed for Holland. However, the chapter of illnesses had only just begun. First Nannerl, then Wolfgang, became ill with intestinal typhoid. They were nursed for many months by their parents and Nannerl became so ill that she was given the last rites.

Eventually they both recovered and were able to continue their tour performing in Utrecht, Amsterdam, Antwerp, Brussels and Munich, before finally returning home to Saltzburg on 29th November 1766.

The whole experience had been deemed a great success. They were famous throughout the Courts of northern Europe. They had earned a great deal of money, more than Leopold would ever admit to, and were the possessors of a dazzling collection of gifts.

Father Hübner, librarian at St. Peter's Abbey in Saltzburg wrote of these tributes – *"of gold watches he has brought home nine: of gold snuff-boxes he has received 12; of gold rings set with the most precious stones he has so many that he does not know himself; ear-rings for the girl, necklaces, knives, bottle holders, writing tackle, toothpick boxes, gold objets for the girl, writing tablets and such gewgaws without end; ----- it is just like inspecting a church treasury."*

The next three years appear to have been a struggle in terms of work and health, for the family. The children survived yet another illness, small pox, and Leopold returned to his orchestral post whilst continually searching for tour opportunities.

Although it seemed that they had made a fortune, travelling had proved expensive, a great deal of time had been wasted waiting for invitations and payment from the nobility, and the weeks and months that Leopold and the children had been laid low with serious illnesses meant that they had earned nothing at all.

Finally Leopold's planning came to fruition. A new tour was arranged, this time to Italy - but only for himself and Wolfgang. He was determined to keep the costs down.

It was the 12th December 1769 when Nannerl saw her father and brother leave for Italy, without her. She was 18 years of age. Her hopes of being able to travel abroad to pursue her own musical training, maybe to Venice as some young women she knew, from Saltzburg, had been allowed to do, had been disregarded. Money was tight and as she was now of marriageable age her place was at home. Her musical gifts and compositions were totally ignored by her father whose only thoughts were on cultivating the greater talent of his son, Wolfgang.

This was the first time that the family had been separated, and for the three trips that were made to Italy over a period of four years Maria Anna and Nannerl had to live the journey through letters. Needless to say, from the correspondence received, they felt great pride in Wolfgang's achievements especially when his first opera, *Mitridate, re di Ponto,* was performed, written when he was only 14 years of age.

Nannerl, at 18 had grown into an attractive young woman, with a keen interest in fashionable clothes and elaborate hairstyles. She caught the eye of several young men including Herr von Mölk who was the son of the Court Chancellor, and Herr von Schiedenhofen.

Leopold approved of these associations as both young men came from respectable Saltzburg families, and allowed Nannerl and her mother to visit the Schiedenhofen country estate at Triebenbach in the Autumn of 1770 and again the following year. This perhaps was considered a treat for the two women, distracting them from the sorrow of being excluded from the tour.

But, even though he was away from home Leopold still demanded regular letters and information on the lives of his two womenfolk, wanting to know whether Nannerl was practising on the harpsichord, and chastising them, especially Anna Maria, quite frequently, for the things they had or had not done.

Wolfgang, on the other hand wrote cheerfully about his experiences, and love of travelling, whilst also encouraging his sister to keep up her music, including composition.

However, the father and son came home, finally, in March 1773, not having created the great opportunities that they had hoped for. Wolfgang's repertoire of compositions and operas was growing, many had been successfully performed, but neither of them had managed to secure for themselves any suitable or rewarding positions. Leopold already suggested, in letters, that Nannerl should consider taking up teaching to help with their depleted finances.

During the year that followed the family decided to move to a larger first floor apartment even though Leopold constantly worried about money. It had formerly belonged to a dancing master, Franz Karl Gottlieb Speckner. There were eight rooms and a small garden at the back. The largest room that had once been a dance studio, was now used for teaching, and for concerts held at home. The Mozart's enjoyed entertaining their friends and in considerable more style than they had before. Visitors also came to view the collection of pianos that Leopold sold, on commission, for outside piano-makers.

In her diary Nannerl records episodes from this final time that they all spent together. She wrote about her daily attendance at Mass, visits that they made, walking with their fox terrier, Bimper, her teaching and the weather. She mentioned public occasions and processions, even exotic events like the arrival of an elephant.

Apart from a trip to Munich where Wolfgang's opera, *La finta giardiniera* was commissioned and performed, a trip in which Nannerl was, surprisingly included, and Anna Maria again, left behind, the family remained in Saltzburg. Both Leopold and Wolfgang were employed at court and Wolfgang had the opportunity to compose many symphonies, string quartets and piano concertos, but, disappointingly, very little opera.

Because of this he was extremely restless, dissatisfied with his unchallenging job that earned him only 150 florins a year, and was desperate to use his talents in the way he desired and make a great deal more money doing it.

So in August 1777 he resigned from his Saltzburg position and left to try his luck elsewhere, travelling first to Augsburg, then Mannheim. He was 21 years of age. His father Leopold was not given leave by Archbishop Colloredo to accompany him, so Anna Maria went instead.

It was not only Nannerl who was upset by once again being left behind, but Leopold also was filled with misery. He described their sorrow in a letter to his wife:

"When we said goodbye, I made great efforts to control myself in order not to make our parting too painful. ----- Nannerl wept bitterly ---- she went off to bed and had the shutters closed. Poor Bimbes (the dog) lay down beside her."

In contrast Anna Maria was thrilled to be travelling again,

although saddened at being parted from her husband and daughter, However Wolfgang still failed to ascend to the heights that he expected, Anna Maria began to feel the loneliness of her isolation from Saltzburg and their lack of money forced them into debt. On the 3rd July 1778, after a mysterious illness, Anna Maria died, in Paris. She was 58 years old.

It was with great sorrow that Wolfgang informed his family back home of her sudden death and he became very depressed at the accusation made by his father that he was somehow to blame, possibly in not calling in the doctor early enough, due to the expense.

In actual fact he coped with the arrangements in a very respectful way. His friend Franz Joseph Heina, a horn player, helped him to organise the funeral, pack up his mother's possessions and send them home to Saltzburg.

Anna Maria had been a dutiful wife and patient, tolerant with her tyrannical husband and steering the fortunes of the family with tact and restraint. Leopold's sorrow at her loss was without question. He wrote to his son, *"Your dear blessed mother was well known from her childhood and loved everywhere, because she was kind to everybody."*

From this time onwards Wolfgang was on his own to pursue his career as he chose. His need for money kept him in contact with home, but he received only censure, advice and endless instructions from his father. He knew that he must return but dawdled, lingering at various places until finally arriving in January 1779. Due to the influence of his father and friends he was given the post of Court organist and concertmaster with a salary of 450 florins. This position kept him in Saltzburg for nearly two years.

During all this time Nannerl still unmarried, remained at home keeping house for her father and brother.

However Wolfgang's spirits were raised when he was commissioned to write an opera for the Elector of Bavaria. When *Idomeneo* was performed in Munich with singers and musicians that he had previously worked with, Leopold and

Nannerl travelled to see it. After an extended trip to Augsburg they returned to Saltzburg, the two men having greatly outstayed their leave of absence.

Archbishop Colloredo demanded that they return to work immediately, Leopold in Saltzburg and Wolfgang in Vienna where the Archbishop was in temporary residence, due to the accession of Joseph II and also because his own father Prince Rudolph Joseph was seriously ill.

After the success of his opera Wolfgang rebelled as he was set to work as a lowly member of the household, and his anger began to flare as he reported in disgust in a letter home that when dining he had to sit *"above the cooks but below the valets."*

Eventually after many arguments between the Archbishop and himself, Wolfgang was reportedly thrown down the stairs and dismissed. His father was appalled and their relationship took a downward turn.

Wolfgang's suggestion that Leopold and Nannerl move to join him in Vienna, where he believed his sister would be able to make a good deal of money playing at private concerts and teaching, was dismissed with disgust. As far as Leopold was concerned his son had brought shame to the family and he and Nannerl were certainly not going to leave their secure life in Saltzburg to satisfy his conscience.

So Wolfgang remained in Vienna. He had broken away from his father's obsessive hold, achieved his own independence and, with Leopold's grudging consent, married Constanze Weber in 1782 and began to build a new career and create a new family.

As for Nannerl she felt trapped. She had never been able to fulfil her musical potential. Her glittering years of childhood were but distant memories. She had been forced to conform to the contemporary status required of young women. Her life of teaching, music making at home and all other activities were under the strict control of her father, and with her mother dead and brother far from home, her life's prospects did not appear at all appealing.

At nearly 30 her chances of being married seemed to be

passing by. In 1780 she had met Franz Armand d'Ippold, who was 22 years her senior. He had been a military captain and then become director of the Collegium Virgilianum in Saltzburg. He is mentioned in Nannerl's diaries during 1781, but it appears that Leopold forced her to turn down his marriage proposal and he withdrew his attentions.

Bouts of illness and tearfulness became common occurrences for Nannerl. Her misery caused angry reactions towards servants, as her life loomed ahead still firmly tethered to her father.

Contact was maintained with Wolfgang through letters both from Nannerl and Leopold. Wolfgang even visited them in Saltzburg in 1783 with his wife Constanze, but the outing was not a success. He could not be forgiven for abandoning them for the excitement of Vienna.

It appears that the brother and sister, who had so thrilled the world with their childhood talent, had drifted apart, never to see each other again.

But finally a suitor came along who proved acceptable to Leopold, and Nannerl was married on the 23rd August 1784. Her bridegroom was Johann Baptist Franz von Berchtold zu Sonnenberg, Prefect of St. Gilgen, as her own maternal grandfather had been.

It is hoped that Nannerl accepted Johann Baptist, as her husband, for the right reasons but it must also be considered that she was desperate to escape from her father's dominance, and maybe, at the age of 33, felt that time was rapidly passing her by. But for whatever reason this marriage enforced a huge change of lifestyle for Nannerl.

Her new husband was 48 years old, a widower twice over. Both his previous wives, Maria and Jeanette, had died in childbirth. Large families and childhood mortality were natural occurrences at the time, and of the 11 babies born to his first two wives, only five survived. Thus Nannerl had not only gained a husband but a family of stepchildren as well.

But one of the delights of her house in St. Gilgen was the coincidence that it had also been the home of her grandmother,

Eva Rosina, and birthplace of her own mother. St. Gilgen was a tiny village on the edge of a lake. When Nannerl arrived that summer it must have seemed so cool and tranquil there, a welcome contrast to the humid heat of Saltzburg.

Sadly the honeymoon period was short. Johann Baptist appeared as overpowering as her father, aloof, unaware of her needs and obviously glad to have a replacement mother for his children, who proved difficult and unruly. Nannerl also had problems in her dealings with servants, as had previously been the case when she'd lived in Saltzburg.

The most depressing part of her new life was the lack of musical activity. She had always been surrounded by it. Her father had generously given her a fortepiano, as a wedding present, but the cold and damp of winter rendered it unplayable.

The only link she had with her former life was the weekly correspondence received from Leopold, and it was through him that she learnt that Wolfgang was prospering, that he and Constanze had moved to a new apartment and greatly wished that his father would go and stay with them, particularly as Constanze had given birth to a son Carl Thomas, born on 21st September, 1784.

In the New Year Leopold decided to make the visit and spent ten weeks in Vienna, enjoying being with his new grandson and basking in Wolfgang's current success. Father and son were once more on good terms and Leopold must have been thrilled at meeting Joseph Hadyn and hearing him extol the talents of his son, *"Before God and as an honest man I tell you that your son is the greatest composer known to me -------- He has taste, and furthermore, the most profound knowledge of composition."*

Nannerl, on the other hand felt totally isolated from her family during that first cold snowy winter at St. Gilgen. Her husband seemed unapproachable, her stepchildren unco-operative and difficult, and she knew no-one interested in music, nor had a functional keyboard to play on.

But there was one piece of good news that she was able to tell her father when she and Johann Baptist travelled to Salzburg to welcome him back from his stay in Vienna. She was going to have a baby.

For some reason it was considered better for Nannerl to give birth in Saltzburg and her father arranged that she travel from St. Gilgen about six weeks prior to the event.

On 27th July 1785 she was delivered safely of a son, Leopold Alois Pantaleon Berchtold. Nannerl remained with her father for another month and then returned home without the baby.

Why she did this is open to speculation. Little Leopold suffered from illness in the first few months of his life and moving him to the cold of St.Gilgen may have seemed unsuitable. Nannerl obviously thought that she would be able to collect him when he was stronger but her own health suffered and she could not. Having five stepchildren to care for could also have been a reason. Leopold, on the other hand probably saw the prospect of raising another genius and was quite content to care for the boy.

In the spring of 1786, however, he wished to go and visit friends in Munich and was most annoyed when Johann Baptist declined to bring Nannerl to Saltzburg to care for little Leopold, because he hadn't the time. When, months later her husband did decide that the journey could be made the little boy was nearly a year old.

In fact Leopold looked after his grandson for nearly two years whilst Nannerl visited him only occasionally.

It would seem that everything good in her life had fallen apart. Her musical career had been forcibly ended, whilst her brother's appeared to be growing in dazzling brilliance, and her father had taken over the care of her own son, due partly, it seems, to the lack of interest taken in him by his own father.

It was only when Leopold died in May 1787, aged 67 that this arrangement changed. Neither Wolfgang nor Nannerl were with their father when he died. Unfortunately after having nursed him for two months Nannerl had returned home, and was not able to arrive back in time, even for the funeral the following evening.

Wolfgang could not afford the cost of travelling home. His yo-

yo fortunes were on a downward trend and his wife was pregnant again.

Leopold's death had a huge effect on his two children. He had been the kingpin of their lives, since childhood. "*After God comes Papa,*" they had recited as children, but there was no doubt that his life had revolved around them and his frustrations with Wolfgang were due to the fact that he'd hoped to nurture his great talent in order to make their fortunes, and had given up his own ambitions to that end.

Cliff Eisen, in The Grove Dictionary writes,

" – *a careful reading in context of the family letters reveals a father who cared deeply for his son but who was frequently frustrated in his greatest ambition: to secure for Wolfgang a wordly position appropriate to his genius.*"

Nannerl had lived with Leopold's irascible tempers and autocratic dominance for nearly 36 years, yet his passing could not help but leave a huge gap in her life. Even after her marriage, in his weekly dispatches he had questioned, in detail, about her family, husband, diet and health and the way she coped with her servants, but now that this communication had ended she felt completely alone in the remoteness of St. Gilgen especially after the will was settled and Wolfgang effectively severed any further relationship with her.

Leopold had left Nannerl his savings - about 3000 florins. The rest of the personal items in his home were to be divided between Wolfgang and herself, to keep or sell. In need of the money Wolfgang could not wait for the results of the auction and demanded a one off payment of 1000 florins and the return of his music. He wanted no personal mementos, kept by his father of their tours and successful early life. This proved to his sister, sadly, that their closeness was well and truly over.

At some time Nannerl dropped her childhood name, and became Marianne and in the next two years she bore two more children, both girls, Johanna (known as Jeanette), on the 22nd March 1789, and Maria Babette on the 17th November 1790. Sadly Maria Babette lived for only six months.

Of the children born to Wolfgang and Constanze only two survived, Carl Thomas born on the 21st September 1784 and Franz Xaver Wolfgang on 26th July 1791. Constanze changed Franz Xaver's name, after her husband's death, to Wolfgang Amadeus, a name that he, as he grew older, found hard to live up to.

It was on 5th December 1791 that their father died, after having been ill since September. He was 35 years old. His widow, Constanze, only 29 herself was left with the two boys, one aged seven, the other a baby of four months. She had no guaranteed income or pension, as Wolfgang had died intestate.

But the family received much support from friends and colleagues. Wolfgang's genius had made a great impact on the musical world even if it had not made his fortune.

How Nannerl came to learn of her brother's death is unknown. However, in 1793, she became involved in an obituary about Wolfgang, compiled by a young German scholar Friedrich von Schlichtegroll, and thus was able to recall many moments of their childhood together.

Von Schlichtegroll was delighted with the intimate knowledge that she gave him, but when the obituary was published a mention of the fact that his marriage to Constanze had been unsuitable caused added animosity between the two women. Constanze is reported to have bought 600 copies of the obituary and destroyed them.

In February, 1801, Nannerl's husband, Johann Baptist, died. He was 65. He had left her financially secure and she was able to leave St.Gilgen and return to her beloved Saltzburg with her children, Leopold, 16 and Jeanette, 12.

She took an apartment in Sigmund-Haffnerstrasse, owned by some old friends, the Barisanis. It was situated just around the corner from her childhood home in Getreidegasse. She then started to give piano lessons again, and began to pick up the threads of her musical life in Saltzburg that she had left behind 17 years earlier.

However tragedy struck when her daughter, Jeanette, died, in 1805 aged only 16, as well as two of her stepchildren. Also, in 1809 her son Leopold was captured and imprisoned, having joined the army to fight the French. Fortunately he survived, was released and left the army, settled in Innsbruch and became a customs officer.

As Nannerl grew older her health began to fail. Although slightly more robust than her brother, her constitution had been weakened by the many illnesses that she had suffered during her childhood and also, to her dismay, she found that she was losing her sight.

But as the years passed and her brother's fame continued to grow and his genius widely acknowledged, her role as his sister began to bring her fame and enjoyment. Many people wanted to meet her and she was able to show them family photographs, memorabilia and accept the growing esteem that was justly hers.

In 1821, when she was 70 she was visited by someone very special, her brother's youngest son Wolfgang, whom she had never met.

Young Wolfgang had inherited his father's wanderlust and travelled a good deal, earning a living as a musician. He was 30 years old when he arrived in Saltzburg and an immediate bond was forged between them. He was thrilled to learn, first hand about the father that he could not remember, about his childhood and parents, Leopold and Anna-Marie, and especially about the early music making successes that his father and Nannerl had experienced.

As for Nannerl she proudly showed him the apartments where they had lived and he was introduced to some of his father's childhood friends who were moved with emotion at meeting him. But for Nannerl her greatest pleasure was gained from listening to him play the piano.

She wrote in her diary:

"In my seventieth year I had the great joy of meeting for the first time the son of my dearly beloved brother. What delightful memories were evoked by hearing him play just as his father had played."

Whenever Wolfgang came to Saltzburg he visited his aunt bringing, without doubt, great joy to her remaining years.

It wasn't long after his first visit that his mother, Constanze, moved to Saltzburg. After having been a widow for 18 years she had married a diplomat, Georg Nissen in 1809. He was completely different, in character, to Wolfgang, solid and reliable, and he adored Constanze. After the turbulence of her former marriage and the struggle of years as a widow she was, in her late forties, more than content to settle into a life of tranquillity with a devoted husband.

Her sons both approved of their new stepfather and spoke of him with respect and affection, grateful that their mother had found happiness once more.

Nissen was Danish, and in 1810 he and Constanze decided to move from Vienna to Copenhagen where he was appointed state press censor, a secure post with a regular salary.

Mozart's music was growing in popularity and the fact that his widow was now living in Copenhagen did not go unnoticed. She had visiting cards made naming both her husbands and regularly invited guests to musical evenings at her home. Once, when her son Wolfgang came to stay, she arranged a concert at the Royal Theatre where she was thrilled to hear him play music written by his brilliant father.

Nissan was a passionate music lover and decided, with Constanze's assistance, to compile a detailed biography of Wolfgang's life and work, but he lacked information that he felt would only be found in Saltzburg. As he approached the age of retirement he made the bold decision to sell up and move.

For Constanze it was a hugely emotional upheaval. She had only visited Saltzburg once before, with Wolfgang, on that less than successful trip in 1783, and the prospect of meeting old acquaintances and especially Nannerl was something that she faced with some trepidation.

However her calm and diplomatic husband, together with her son Wolfgang, helped to smooth the way. Nannerl's pleasure in having met her brother's youngest son naturally warmed her towards the meeting again with his mother, after 40 years.

Working with Nissen, seeing his obvious devotion to

Constanze, Nannerl realised his sincerity for the task and obvious determination to produce a thorough biography. She was able to show him letters, memorabilia and tell him, in detail, about her brother's early life, and as Nannerl's health and eyesight weakened Constanze offered care and support, and the two women, in their declining years, grew closer together.

This huge task, however, was detrimental to Nissen's health. He had barely written the Preface before he was taken ill with, *"paralysis of the lungs"* and died on the 24ᵗʰ March 1826, aged 65.

In Nissen's memory Constanze organised a performance of her first husband's Requiem, conducted by her son, Wolfgang.

Coincidentally the husband of Constanze's sister, Sophie died on the same day and to comfort each other in their loss and loneliness the two sisters decided to move in together in Saltzburg.

Constanze handed over the biography to Johann Friedrich Feuerstein, a doctor of medicine and an old friend of Nissen's who completed it, in a most unsatisfactory way with little shape and poorly written text. After its initial distribution amongst patrons, royalty and friends, the sales dropped and the book was not reprinted for 20 years.

On 10ᵗʰ October 1829 Nannerl died. She was 78 years old and had, in her final years become *"blind, languid, exhausted, feeble and nearly speechless."*

Her early years had been full of glamorous excitement. She had achieved a fame that few children have ever been known to accomplish, yet she'd been forced to realise that her undoubted musical talent was not considered as great as that of her brother. She'd succumbed to moments of jealousy as well as proudly acknowledging his brilliance, and, with modesty, she had declared, *"I am only my brother's pupil."*

For 50 years of her life she had been dominated, organised and influenced by three men, her father, brother and husband.

Her father, Leopold, at first, had encouraged her musical ability until her brother's genius had become apparent, then he'd practically ignored her, showing no consideration for her wishes. Her adult life had been lived in domestic subordination particularly after the death of her mother. Her music making had been restricted to home entertainment, and none of her compositions have survived.

She was very close to her brother in her early years and sincerely admired his talent and desire to excel. He had always been considerate to her, had known how she'd longed for the opportunities that were his, and had written many pieces for her to play, sending them to her when he was away travelling.

He'd wanted her to be happily married, as he was, but his success in escaping from the dominance of his father, and her lack of being able to and seemingly siding with Leopold against him, had caused the separation between them that was never repaired.

Johann Baptist, her husband had also shown little concern for her needs and it wasn't long before Nannerl realised that she had escaped one form of domestic slavery for another. But, she had made her choice, settled for her lot, won over her stepchildren and become a good and caring mother to them as well as to her own children.

Only in her final years did she find peace to live, as a widow, in Saltzburg, with her children, and the joy that had begun her life returned in the musical life and teaching that she was able to rekindle.

It must have been wonderful for her to relive her early years through her nephew Wolfgang and to realise the continual world wide growth of the amazing musical legacy left by her brother, in his short lifetime.

Would Nannerl, given the same opportunities, have also flourished as a performer and composer? In our modern age the choice would have been hers, but in the 18th century, prospects, independence and the right of a career were not available to women. Thus whatever Maria "Nannerl" Mozart and others like her might have accomplished musically, is left totally to speculation.

6. Fanny Hensel, 1842, by Moritz Daniel Oppenheim

7. Fanny Mendelssohn, sketched by her future husband Wilhelm Hensel

8. Portrait of Mendelssohn
by the English miniaturist
James Warren Childe
(1778–1862), 1839

Chapter 2

Fanny Mendelssohn

1805 - 1847

"Perhaps music will be his profession, whereas for you it can and must be but an ornament and never the fundamental bass line of your existence and activity."

Abraham Mendelssohn 16th July 1820.

This excerpt comes from a letter written to Fanny by her father Abraham at a time when, at the age of 15, she was emerging as a remarkable pianist and had already written many compositions.

She had shared an excellent education with her brother Felix, was considered to have considerable musical talent, but because of her female status her father denied her the opportunity to further her training and become a professional musician.

"You must prepare for your real calling, the only calling of a young woman – I mean the state of a housewife."

It appears that very little had changed in the status and expectancy of women in the intervening years between the longings of a youthful Nannerl Mozart and those of Fanny Mendelssohn.

Fanny was born in the year that Nannerl reached the age of 54. Nannerl, a widow for four years, returned to her beloved Saltzburg after the death of her husband and was able to live near her old home and earn a living by teaching the piano.

Both Nannerl and Fanny had prodigious musical talent recognised immediately by their fathers, Leopold and Abraham. They were allowed the same education as their younger brothers but as Wolfgang and Felix grew, and their musical geniuses became evident, so the limelight in which their older sisters had basked, faded, and they had to resort to the roles expected of women, living out their musical dreams within the seclusion of their own permitted environment.

However, their backgrounds were innately dissimilar, the Mozart's existence being plagued by lack of money; the Mendelssohn's comfortable middle-class life style deriving from a successful family banking business.

Sadly the closeness between Wolfgang and Nannerl did not survive, whereas that between Felix and Fanny was constant and lasting. Nannerl's marriage seemed to have been fraught with difficulties; Fanny's was built on love and contentment and her sudden death, at the age of 42, left her husband and brother devastated.

Fanny Caecilie Mendelssohn was born on November 14th 1805. She was the daughter of Abraham and Leah Mendelssohn Bartholdy, and older sister of Felix, Rebecka and Paul.

Her place of birth was Hamburg where the family lived in a cottage called *Martin's Mill* with a balcony overlooking the river Elbe. Prophetically Abraham, on informing his mother-in-law, Madame Salomon, of Fanny's birth is quoted as saying, *"Leah says that the child has Bach-fugue fingers."*

It was evident that she had been born into a family endowed with great intelligence and talent. The four children were the culmination of a remarkable heritage that was manifested in the genius of their brother Felix.

Abraham's comment, *"Formerly, I was the son of my father; now, I am the father of my son,"* aptly describes his pride in both.

The father of whom he spoke was Moses Mendelssohn born, a Jew, on September 6th 1729, into a poor family living in a crowded and squalid ghetto in Dessau. His father, Mendal, was a teacher in the religious school held in the synagogue, and he would take young Moses with him to make sure that he had every opportunity to learn. It was when he realised that his son possessed an exceptional ability that he passed his education on to Rabbi Frankel who was distinguished for his intellectual freedom and knowledge.

But opportunities were restricted for Jewish boys especially a frail, undersized boy like Moses with a permanent curvature of the spine that left him unfit for manual labour. The only occupation open to him was that of a pedlar, selling merchandise from village to village, and when Rabbi Frankel moved to Berlin as *Oberrabbiner* (head rabbi) Moses, at the young age of 14 decided to follow him. The Jewish entrance into Berlin was through the Rosenthal Gate, and when he was asked, "*What is your business?*" he replied, "*I have come to learn.*"

For seven years he lived in poverty. Frankel found him work as a copyist and during these years he absorbed everything he could. He became a self-educated man, expert in mathematics, languages and philosophy.

In particular he learnt German, forbidden by the Jewish community, realising that this was the only way to emerge from his ghetto background. He was the first person to call himself a German Jew, changing his name from Moses Dessau to Moses Mendelssohn meaning Moses, son of Mendal.

At the age of 21 he was engaged as a tutor to the four children of a Jewish silk merchant, Isaac Bernhard, for whom he also kept the books and dealt with customers. Every evening he would meet friends and talk about literature, politics and his own philosophy on life and he gradually developed a flourishing career as a critic and writer earning himself the nickname of the *German Socrates*.

In 1762, at the age of 33 he married Fromet Gugenheim. They had three sons and three daughters of whom Abraham (1776 –1835) was their second son. Abraham and his elder brother, Joseph, built up a banking business, *Mendelssohn and Company* that lasted until 1939, when the Nazis closed it down.

Moses died in January 1786 at the age of 56, his legacy a lifetime's work of initiating the Jewish race into modern times, his name linked with a firm belief in the power of thought, reason and knowledge.

Fanny, his granddaughter was eminently proud of her ancestral heritage, even though she had inherited her grandfather's curvature of the spine.

Although Abraham considered himself a *bridge* between his father and son he was a man of character and intellect with a keenness to investigate new places and ideas. Financially Moses had left his family in a situation that was not particularly secure so, deciding on a banking career, Abraham moved to Paris, in 1797, to work in Fould's Bank on the Rue Bergère.

He met and married Leah Salomon (1777–1842), granddaughter of Daniel Itzig, a member of one of Berlin's privileged Jewish Families. Leah had been well educated, spoke three languages, was musical, artistic, and very rich. Thus it was that Abraham, with capital behind him, was able to go into partnership with his brother, Joseph, and open a family bank.

His three oldest children were born in Hamburg, Felix four years after Fanny in 1809 and Rebecka in 1811. Paul was born in 1812 after the family had moved to Berlin.

It was Leah who instigated that they should be baptised as Christians. She felt that they would integrate and be more readily accepted into the German community if they became Lutherans. She eventually persuaded her reluctant husband, and the children were baptised in 1816 when Fanny was 11 and Felix seven. They were urged by Leah's brother, Jacob to take on the name of Bartholdy as he had, instead of Mendelssohn, something that the children fought against. In the end a compromise was reached and both names were adopted, although Felix was adamant and retained the name Mendelssohn throughout his life.

Education took a prominent role in the lives of all four children. Abraham was so fired up with ambition that he woke them every morning at five o'clock to begin their morning's lessons. Both parents were excellent amateur musicians and Leah became their first piano teacher, sitting in the same room, knitting, as each child practised.

Abraham engaged many tutors, the most notable being Carl Friedrich Zelter, a skilled musician and director of Berlin's finest institution for choral music called the *Singakademie.* He was well known as a composer of songs set to the poetry of Johann Wolfgang von Goethe.

Zelter introduced the children to the music of J.S. Bach, Mozart and Beethoven. Fanny was so impressed by Bach's music that she memorised 24 of his preludes, when she was only 13, as a surprise for her father.

He also appointed the eminent pianist, Ludwig Berger, as piano tutor and Karl Heyse as a general tutor.

As a result of this superb instruction, the children became outstanding scholars, Fanny and Felix especially, showing remarkable musical talent and composing a variety of pieces at a very early age.

It was hard for the two younger children, Rebecka and Paul, to assert themselves. They were not considered to be as musically gifted as their older brother and sister although Rebecka had a sweet singing voice, and Paul played the 'cello well enough for Felix to compose several pieces for him.

At first Fanny, being the oldest, lorded it over her younger brothers and sister, showing off her virtuosity, This was not always to their liking and may be the reason why Felix, years later, after he had become internationally known, took on the role of his late father and declined to help Fanny publish her compositions.

However Felix and Fanny's relationship was strongly built on their love of music and appreciation of each other's talents. Fanny is quoted as saying, *"I have always been his musical adviser and he never writes down a thought before submitting it to my judgement - I have known his operas by heart before a note was written."*

There was no doubt that her enthusiasm to be an accomplished musician and composer, like her brother, was of paramount importance to her. Her first known composition, *Songs, fly joyously away,* was written in 1819, in honour of her father's birthday. It exhibited the spontaneity and melodic inspiration that is a characteristic of her style.

In 1820 at the age of 15 she enrolled at the *Singakademie* in Berlin.

She wrote many songs and piano pieces during this period, scribbling them into manuscript books. Some of her melodic piano pieces were written under the name of *Songs without words.* Felix, of course, is well known for his compositions of that name and it is unsure which of the siblings first created the title.

However it became apparent, as Felix grew older, that the tutors nurtured his progress, more than Fanny's.

It was at this time, 1819 –1820 that her father Abraham who was away from home, in Paris, decided that it was high time for Fanny's *"wings to be clipped."* She must be made to understand her duty, consider the life she was expected to lead in devotion to her family and begin to create her future role as wife and mother.

Felix, on the other hand was steadily progressing towards becoming a professional musician. As a performer he gave his first public concert at the age of nine and by the age of 11 had composed at least 60 works ranging from songs and piano pieces to trios for piano, violin and cello.

Their parents, mainly to promote Felix, began giving concerts at home, called *Sonntagsmusiken* (Sunday Musicales). These began in 1823 in their first Berlin home on the New Promenade and then in the spacious residence at No. 3 Leipziger Strasse. Abraham hired musicians to play works by contemporary as well as established composers, and also gave both Felix and Fanny the chance to perform their own compositions to selected guests, in a semi-public setting.

During this time Fanny, due to her domestic restrictions, wrote mostly piano pieces and songs. In her desperation to become known outside the inner circle of family friends Felix agreed to allow her to publish five songs and a duet under his own name, in his *Liederheften, Opus 8 & 9.* The duet is considered to be the finest piece in the collection.

One of the songs, *Italy*, when performed later, on one of his trips to England, became a favourite of Queen Victoria, and Felix was obliged to admit to the great lady that, in fact, his sister had written it.

Fanny continued to compose even though both her father and Felix would not support her in her efforts to have her music published under her own name.

When she was 17 she met Wilhelm Hensel, a young and talented artist. He had been born in the German town of Trebbin on July 6th 1794 where his father was a protestant preacher. His interests had initially been in the study of architecture but after a spell in military service he discovered his true passion, painting.

He was immediately won over by Fanny's spirit and in particular her magnificent dark eyes. There was no way that marriage could be considered between them. She was too young and he was virtually penniless.

However his painting of scenes that had previously been represented as a tableaux, so pleased the Grand Duke Nicholas of Bavaria and his wife that they agreed to provide him with a scholarship to study in Rome. Thus it was that Wilhelm left for Italy, in 1825, where he was to spend five years, with no promise of an engagement by Fanny's family. The two lovers were not even allowed to correspond, but he did communicate with Leah, sending portraits of her children, created from memory, many of course of Fanny, causing her motherly resolve to soften towards him.

It was in this same year of 1825 that the Mendelssohn family moved to No.3 Leipziger Strasse. The house was large and stately, roomy enough for the performance of their musical soirées, plays, tableaux and operettas.

The garden was described by Leah to Wilhelm as, *"quite a park, with splendid trees, a field, grass-plots, and a delightful summer residence."* This residence was, in fact, a rambling, one-storied garden house, bitterly cold in winter but a paradise in summer. It was here that Wilhelm and Fanny set up home, after they were married.

So many friends were welcomed into this new mansion

including Karl Klingemann, author of the words of Felix's opera, *Son and Stranger*, Eduard Rietz, a violinist, Adolph Bernhard Marx, the editor of a musical paper and the poet Heinrich Heine. They absorbed the musical ethos of the family and read and discussed currently popular works such as Jean Paul and Shakespeare.

For Felix this setting with its walks, shady paths, old trees and seasonal flowers was the stimulus that inspired his *Overture to a Midsummer Night's Dream.*

The two sisters were greatly admired although Rebecka is quoted as saying that, *"My older brother and sister stole my reputation as an artist."*

However, she was considered to be prettier and more amusing than Fanny and Heine claimed he only visited when he knew that Rebecka would be at home.

It was into this close cultural scene that Wilhelm Hensel returned, in 1828. He was now 34 and Fanny almost 23. He found it difficult to integrate into the intellectual community that had developed between Fanny's family and their intimate friends. He was not musical himself, became jealous of her closeness to others, and caused Fanny to question her reasons for deciding to marry him.

It was through his Art that Wilhelm eventually broke into the close circle that surrounded the two sisters, known as *"The Wheel."* He drew an actual wheel with Felix as the hub and all the other members of the society as the spokes. He also drew himself chained to the outside, the chain being held by Fanny. The significance of this had its effect. His Art was appreciated and he was accepted not only into the close union of friends but also as Fanny's prospective husband.

Their formal betrothal took place in January 1829, a month before Felix left for England on the first of his ten visits.

Fanny's wedding took place on October 3rd 1829, without Felix. He had badly damaged his knee in a traffic accident in London when his carriage overturned, and for two months he had to endure rest in bed. Apart from his own annoyance he realised that Fanny would be very upset that he couldn't be at her wedding and sent an affectionate letter in which he said, *"For the last time I address you as Miss Fanny Mendelssohn Bartholdy - Live and prosper, get married and be happy; shape your household so that I shall find you in a beautiful home when I come."*

On the morning of her wedding she wrote to him, *"I have your portrait before me - thinking of you as if you stood by my side - every moment of my life I shall love you from the bottom of my heart."*

The wedding was a beautiful occasion and Fanny walked down the aisle to music that she had composed herself. She appeared happy and confident, looking forward to her life with a man who obviously adored her.

Wilhelm's appointment as professor at the Academy of Fine Arts, in February 1829, had been greatly to his favour in the eyes of his future parents-in-law, but, as he was unable to guarantee the standard of living that Fanny was used to he was indebted to her family when they were offered a home, in a wing of the garden house. The building was rather cold and dark but Abraham remodelled it for them ordering walls to be knocked down so that the sunlight could invade the dampness.

A large studio was made for Wilhelm where he happily settled to paint, and, in 1831 began to teach students, thus adding to his spasmodic income that relied on sales of paintings and occasional royal commissions.

The Hensel's settled comfortably into their *Gartenhaus*. Wilhelm's studio opened onto the music room, and as he painted he could hear Fanny at her piano, playing and composing.

In 1830 Fanny gave birth to a son and named him after her three favourite composers, Sebastian Ludwig Felix. These names were hard for Sebastian to cope with when he started school. He was quite small and strangely dressed and it took all his self-confidence to assert himself.

The pregnancy had not been straightforward. There had been a threat of a miscarriage and Sebastian had been born prematurely. He was weak and his chances of survival were slender. However he thrived due to the loving care he received, especially from Wilhelm, and within a few months was as fat and healthy as any parents could wish.

Sebastian proved to be their only child. Fanny had a series of miscarriages that left her weakened both physically and mentally. Her mother and husband tried to encourage her to play and compose, but she found herself greatly lacking in creative motivation. It didn't help when Felix wrote her a letter in which he expressed surprise that, with a young baby, Fanny could even contemplate anything other than being a doting mother.

An outbreak of cholera, in Berlin in 1831 caused many deaths. Fanny was a lucky survivor but many of her friends succumbed and over a period of two years she listed in her diary 13 people, close to her, who had died for one reason or another. Included in this list were the violinist Rietz and their old tutor Zelter.

Hearing of Zelter's death Felix had hopes of stepping into his shoes as the conductor of the Berlin Singakademie. However the post was given to Karl Rungenhagen, who had been Zelter's assistant. He was 30 years older than Felix, a composer with no desire to go travelling. Felix supposed that this choice was made because he was considered to be too young. It is more likely however that his Jewish origins swung the decision against him.

It was in the Spring of 1831 that Fanny, encouraged by Wilhelm, reinstated her Sunday musical matinees that took place in her parlour with Wilhelm's studio on one side, and the garden terrace on the other. These matinees became a focus for her musical energies and were prestigious enough to attract the attendance of several members of the aristocracy as well as other rising figures in the artistic world.

She introduced her audience to music composed by Beethoven, Bach, Mozart, Weber and, of course, her brother Felix. She presented her own songs and piano pieces, conducted a choir of 20 singers and welcomed visiting artistes such as Liszt, Clara Schumann, Paganini and Heine.

As an amateur activity these concerts were a great outlet for her abundant talents, enriched the lives of the people involved, and temporarily made up for the restrictions she encountered from her father and brother.

Fanny and Wilhelm's house became the central hub of a wider *"wheel"*. Artists, musicians, and singers, as well as authors and scientists were all drawn and welcomed into this cultural setting, and whilst they made music, talked and discussed, Wilhelm sketched them informally. The resulting drawings, on his death, filled 47 volumes and contained almost a thousand portraits uniquely autographed by those pictured within.

There is no doubt that Fanny's musical salon was a great success during the 1830's and her many compositions began to include larger works. Some of these were cantatas, for soloists, choir and orchestra, *Hiob, Lobgesang and Oratorium*.

Yet Fanny could not help but be disillusioned when she compared her life with that of her brother. Felix was becoming famous throughout Europe, able to travel and experience a musical life in London, Vienna and Paris, whilst she must remain at home, in seeming isolation.

In 1836 she wrote to a close friend, *"If no-one ever offers an opinion, or takes the slightest interest in one's production, one loses in time not only all pleasure in them, but all power of judging their value. Felix, who is alone a sufficient public for me, is so seldom here that he cannot help me much, thus I am thrown back entirely upon myself"*.

Her sister Rebecka in part, added to this general depression, as she no longer wished to sing for Fanny. In May 1832 Rebecka had married Gustav Peter Lejeune Dirichlet, a young Belgian scientist and mathematician, and her first child, Walter had been born in 1833. Rebecka and Gustav also lived, for a while, in an apartment at 3 Leipziger Strasse but moved out because they felt it was too cold.

Abraham and Leah took some persuading to allow another impoverished suitor into the family, even though Dirichlet's genius resulted in his eventually becoming a foremost figure in the field of mathematics.

In 1835 Abraham, who was almost completely blind, caught a cold and died in his sleep. Felix had, in the same year, been appointed conductor of the Leipzig Gewandhaus Orchestra. For some time he had been writing a choral work on the life of St. Paul, and this he finished and dedicated to the memory of his father. This large-scale work had its first performance in May 1836, at the Lower Rhine Festival in Dusseldorf. Members of the family travelled there for the premiere, and Fanny sang in the chorus.

Felix, at the age of 27 was now the only one of Abraham and Leah's children to be still unmarried. Paul, his younger brother, who had become a banker, had recently married Albertine Heine, cousin of Heinrich Heine, the poet.

Felix was, actually more than ready to settle down and when he met Cecile Jeanrenaud, a talented painter and amateur singer, he wasted no time in courting her. Cecile who was only 18 and acknowledged as one of the most beautiful girls in Frankfurt was, at first, rather in awe of her famous suitor.

Their wedding took place on the 28th March 1837 after which Felix became a settled home-loving husband, determined to make his wife feel welcome in the Mendelssohn family circle. During their ten years of marriage Cecile bore five children, Carl, Marie, Paul, Felix and Lili, but, sadly, little Felix did not survive, and died in infancy.

So the roles of the family were reversed. Felix, who was happily settled in Leipzig, preferred to stay at home with his family whilst his two sisters had, at last, a chance to travel.

Fanny, Wilhelm and Sebastian spent a whole year in Italy from September 1839 to the following September. They visited Milan, Venice, Florence and Rome absorbing the culture and history of some of the most famous places in the world.

This was one of the happiest years of Fanny's life. She had finally escaped her semi-prison, was able to compose and perform her work outside her home environment, and received recognition from a variety of other musicians, including Gounod, Massenet and Berlioz. Their respect and patronage greatly boosted her confidence.

The years following her return were notable for the surge of compositions that her successful journey had inspired. The most impressive of these was a piano work, *Das Jahr, (The Year)*. This was written as a memory of her year spent in Italy, and consisted of 12 pieces, one for each month, finishing with a final chorale that was her harmonisation of a Lutheran melody.

In 1841 Felix and his family returned to Berlin. He had been engaged to work for the new King of Prussia, Frederick William IV. His presence greatly added to the brilliance of Fanny's Sunday Musicales, and she was glad that they were together to share the sadness of the death of their mother Leah, in 1842.

But Felix was not happily employed, and after five years in the King's service resigned and returned to Leipzig. Fanny was very upset at losing his companionship and that of Cecile and her children. She had hoped that they would have *"grown old together."*

However she continued to play and compose and in 1846 her mentor became Robert von Keudell, who was a diplomat, musically talented and well educated. She said of him, *"he keeps me breathless and in a constant state of musical activity."*

It was Keudell who influenced her to go against the wishes that her father and brother had formerly expressed, and accept an offer to publish her work. She had the choice of two publishing houses and the full support of her husband. Only one other person's encouragement was vital to this project. She needed Felix to approve.

So she broached the subject in a letter, *"Since I know in advance that you won't be pleased, I'll go about this awkwardly. Laugh at me, if you like, but at the age of forty I'm as afraid of my brother as I was of Father when I was fourteen - In a word I'm beginning to publish."*

Felix took a whole month to reply but when he did it was to give his *"professional blessing upon your decision to enter our guild, - may you know only the pleasures of being a composer, and none of the miseries - may the public only send you roses."*

Fanny was encouraged by this response although she still felt that in his heart he was still not totally won over.

It was during the winter of 1846/7 that Robert and Clara Schumann stayed in Berlin and added their talents and compositions to the Sunday Musicales. Fanny and Clara were immediately drawn to each other. *"I have really taken a liking to Frau Hensel,"* wrote Clara, *"and feel particularly drawn to her musically."*

She greatly admired Fanny's piano playing but was more conservative with her attitude towards publication. She realised how hard it was for women to be accepted professionally. *"Women as composers cannot deny themselves as women, and I say this of myself as much as of the others."*

Clara whilst her husband was alive, kept her considerable ability as a composer reined, although her father had always intended his daughter to compose and perform. This was greatly in contrast to Fanny's experiences as a musician, having to forge her way through the obstacles that Abraham and Felix created.

Yet Fanny would not be deterred. Her publishers were Bote und Bock of Berlin and her published works were a mixture of solo songs, piano pieces and four part harmonies for soprano, contralto, tenor and bass.

In January 1847 critical reviews began to appear in the *Neue Zeitschrift für Musik*, the paper that Robert Schumann had founded, in Leipzig. The comments voiced a surprise that the compositions were not bad. It seemed that, at this present time, no critic wanted to admit that women could write music that was both imaginative and creative.

"We shall reserve a more detailed and general judgement until familiar with other works by the composer."

Fanny was not dismayed and began work on her *Trio in D Minor* for piano, violin and cello. It was to be her masterpiece, written in celebration of Rebecka's birthday on 11th April and its debut opened her new season of Sunday Musicales in the garden room.

The tide was turning in Fanny's favour. Her home life was settled and happy and her work was reaping rewards. One of the last entries in her diary was in 1847, as the cold of winter began to give way to the freshness of Spring.

"Yesterday," she wrote, *" the first breath of Spring was in the*

air. It has been a long winter, with much frost and snow - when in the morning, after breakfasting with Wilhelm, we each go to our own work with a pleasant day to look back upon and another to look forward to, I am quite overcome with my own happiness."

For several years Fanny had suffered from nosebleeds. They were not considered important at the time but may have been a warning sign to her sudden and early death.

On the afternoon of May 14th 1847 she was sitting at the piano rehearsing with her choir for the Sunday performance of Felix's *Walpurgis Night.* It was a hot and sultry day and Fanny, who often suffered from high blood pressure, felt her arms go numb. The paralysis worsened and, recognising the symptoms, she said, *"It's a stroke, like mother had."* Eventually she could not move or speak, became unconscious and died later that evening, her death caused by a cerebral haemorrhage. She was 41 years old.

The family were devastated by the suddenness of this tragedy. Instead of the Sunday concert her coffin was laid in the garden room, surrounded by flowers, for her friends to come and pay their respects. Wilhelm drew a last and most perfect portrait of her and from then onwards he painted nothing of worth. His love and inspiration had gone. He resigned all his commissions, lived for another 15 years, devoting himself to politics.

When Fanny died part of Felix died too. He never really recovered from the shock of her death. In spirit and mind they had been like identical twins. It is thought that on hearing the news he may have suffered a minor stroke. He tried to keep working but his heart was not in it. He was incapable of returning to Berlin for Fanny's funeral. He felt ill, fatigued, was weakened by headaches and fainting spells and died on November 4th, from a stroke, less than six months after the death of his sister.

He was buried beside Fanny in the churchyard of the Holy Trinity. Wilhelm, later, was buried on her other side.

Sebastian was 17 when his mother died, and after the death also, of his uncle he became seriously ill. When he recovered he went to live with his Aunt Rebecka. He did not become an artist or musician but a landowner, businessman and author. He married Julie von Adelson and they had five children.

His most famous work was, *The Family Mendelssohn, 1729 -1847*, compiled from the large number of family letters and journals that he had inherited. It was first published in 1879.

Sebastian described his mother thus, *"Her finest features were her eyes, which were large, sombre and very expressive, with a short sightedness people did not notice. Her nose and mouth were quite pronounced and she had beautiful white teeth. That she often practiced the piano showed in her hands. She was lively and decided in her movements."* -

"I have never seen anyone who so intensely enjoyed anything beautiful: a fine day, handsome people, a wonderful talent, a beautiful landscape. She would gulp in fresh air to the bottom of her lungs." -

"She was quite indifferent to material wealth: good food and drink, comfort, clothes, luxury of any kind. None of this was necessary to her life; on the other hand, she could not live without the company of a small circle of cultivated, intelligent people, or without the pleasures of art."

Death came to Fanny just as the outside world was beginning to open its doors to her as a composer. She was almost 40 before her first piano pieces and songs were published. After her death Felix had several more of her works published making a total of 11 opus numbers.

For well over a hundred years her music lay dormant, held by her family or in the archives of the Berlin State Library.

In the 1990's some of her manuscripts began to emerge. A four-disc set was issued on Germany's CPO label and three volumes of her vocal and keyboard music on the Thorofon label. However, even at the beginning of the 21st century much of her work is still inaccessible.

In 1996 Allan Kozinn, reviewer in the New York Times, heard the piece, *Das Jahr*, and wrote, *"This is an outgoing cycle: even the ruminative, bittersweet serenades, June and July, grow into densely textured virtuoso works, and most of the pieces have more of (Robert) Schumann's audaciousness than Felix Mendelssohn's delicacy."*

It began to seem that Fanny's musical compositions were, at last, being compared favourably with that of her brother.

Stephen Albert, Pulitzer prize-winning composer, when asked to comment on Fanny's *Piano Trio* of 1846 said, *"She's certainly more adventurous than her brother. She's plenty talented. There's a clarity of thought, a real inevitability to her music."*

Composer Gunther Schuller remarked, " *– she was extremely prolific, but on a very high, consistent level. The kind of thing where you say, "Why don't we know this music better?"*

Fanny composed over 400 pieces of music.

There was no doubt that she had been very skilled at combining piano and voice. She wrote beautiful melodies and, as she herself was a formidable pianist her accompaniments were demanding and skilful. Sincerity and emotion shone out, giving it a unique and joyful atmosphere. It is unfortunate that so much music of this quality is still unavailable.

Fanny did not complete her life's work nor did she reach her full potential. To be considered a genius was a male prerogative and to attempt to perform and compose professionally, on a par with men, was acting against all the prevailing attitudes, at the time, towards the role expected of women.

Published Works by Fanny Mendelssohn

Instrumental Music

Chamber Music

Adagio for Violin and Piano. Rosario Marciano, ed. Furore, Kassel, 1989.

Piano Quartet in A flat major. Renate Eggebrecht-Kupsa, ed. Furore, Kassel, 1990

*Piano Trio in D minor, Op 11.*Wollenweber, Gräfelfing, 1984.

String Quartet in E flat major. Renate Eggebrecht-Kupsa, ed. Furore, Kassel, 1988

String Quartet in E flat major. Günter Marx, ed. Breitkopf & Härtel, Wiesbaden, 1989

Music for Piano

"*Abschied von Rom*"
" *Il saltarello romano*" *Opus 6 No.4*
"*Notturno*"
"*O Traum der Jugend, o goldener Stern.*"
In *At the Piano with Felix and Fanny Mendelssohn.* Maurice Hinson, ed. Alfred Publishing, Sherman Oaks, CA, 1990

Two Bagatelles for Piano. Barbara Heller, ed. Furore, Kassel, 1988

"*Das Jahr,*" Twelve Character Pieces for the Pianoforte, vols. 1 and 2. Barbara Heller and Liana Gavrila Serbescu, eds. Furore,

Kassel, 1989.

Songs for the Pianoforte, Op. 2
Pastorella, Op.6.
Bote and Bock, Berlin, 1983.

Four Songs without Words for Piano, Op.8. Eva Rieger, ed.
Furore, Kassel, 1989.

Six Melodies for the Piano, Op.4 and Op. 5. Lienau, Berlin, 1982.

Melodies, Op.4. Nos. 2 and 4. In Frauen Komponieren.
22 Klavierstücke des 18-20. Jahrhunderts.
Eva Rieger, ed. Schott, Mainz, 1985.

Melody for Piano. Op.4, No. 2. In At the Piano with Women
Composers.
Melody for piano, Op. 5. No. 4
Maurice Hinson, ed. Alfred publishing, Sherman Oaks CA, 1990

Prelude for Piano. Rosario Marciano, ed. Furore, Kassel, 1989

Sonata in G minor for Piano. Barbara Heller and Liana Gavrila
Serbescu eds. Furore, Kassel, 1991

Sonata in C minor.
Sonata Movement in E major.
Barbara Heller and Liana Gavrila Serbescu, eds. Furore Kassel,
1991

Sonata in C minor In Two Piano Sonatas
Sonata in G minor
Judith Radell, ed. Hildegard Publishing, Bryn Mawr, PA, 1992
Three Pieces for Four-hand piano. Barbara Gabler, ed. Furore,
Kassel, 1990
Two Etudes

Two untitled piano pieces
"Notturno"
"Abschied von Rom"
Allegro Molto
Andante Cantabile
"O Traum der Jugend, o goldener Stern"
Allegretto
Allegro Vivace
In Ausgewahlte Klavierwerke Fanny Kistner-Hensel, ed. Henle, Munich, 1986

Music for Organ

Organ Prelude. Elke Mascha Blankenburg, ed. Furore, Kassel, 1988

Vocal Music.

Lieder for voice and piano

Selected Songs; *"Sehnsucht nach Italien," "Mignon," "In die Ferne," "Sehnsucht," "Anklänge 2," "Anklänge 3," "Traurige Wege," "Auf dem See," "Liebe in der Fremde."* Edition Donna. Düsseldorf, 1991.

Selected Songs, vol 1; *"Wander lied," Op 2, No.2; "Warum sind denn die Rosen so blass," Op 1 No. 3; "Morgenständchen, Op.1 No. 5; "Nacht-wanderer," Op. 7. No.1; "Frühling," Op.7, No.3; "Die frühen Gräber,"Op. 9, No.4; "Die Mainacht," Op. 9, No.6; "Nach Süden," Op. 10, No.1; "Vorwurf," Op.10, No.2; "Abendbild," Op.10, No 3; "Im Herbste," Op.10, No.4; "Bergeslust," Op. 10, No. 5; "Die Schiffende," "Kein Blick der Hoffnung," 2 Der Eichwald*

brauset."
Breitopf 7 Härtel, Wiesbaden, 1994.

Selected Songs, vol. 2: *"Traurige Wege," "Dämmerung senkte sich von oben," "Uber allen Gipfeln ist Ruh," "Wandrers Nachtlied," "An Suleika," "Suleika," "Ach, die Augen sind es wieder," "Fichtenbaum und Palme," "Nacht ist wie ein stilles Meer," "Ich kann wohl manchmal singen," "Im Herbst," "Anklänge 1-3."*
Breitkopf & Härtel, Wiesbaden,1993.

Sixteen Songs. John Glenn Paton,ed. Alfred Publishing Co., Inc., Van Nuys, CA, 1995.

Songs, Op. 1 and Op. 7. Bote & Bock, Berlin, 1985.

Songs, Op. 9 and Op. 10. Breitkopf & Härtel, 1850.

Songs in *Felix Mendelssohn-sämtliche Lieder*: *"Das Heimweh," Op. 8, No. 2; "Italien," Op. 8, No. 3; "Sehnsucht," Op. 9, No. 7; "Verlust," Op. 9, No. 10; "Die Nonne," Op. 9, No. 12.*
Edition Peters, Frankfurt.

Works for Chorus a capella

"Morgengruss," Op. 3, No. 4, for four-part chorus a capella.
Breitkopf & Härtel, Wiesbaden.

Choral movements for four-part chorus a capella: *"Abendlich schon rauscht der Wald," Op. 3, No. 5; "Druben geht die Sonne scheiden," "Horst du nicht die Bäume rauschen," Op. 3, No. 1; "O Herbst, in linden Tagen," 2 Schweight der Menschen laute Lust."*
In *Chorbuch Romantik.* Möseler, Wolfenbüttel, 1988.
Choral movements for four-part chorus a capella: *"Fruhzeitiger*

Fruhling,"
"Unter des Laubdachs Hut."
Joachim Draheim, ed. Breitkopf & Härtel, Wiesbaden, 1989.

Choral movements for four-part mixed chorus a capella: *"Schöne Fremde,"*
"Es rauschen die Wipfel."
Joachim Draheim, ed. Breitkopf & Härtel, Wiesbaden, 1990.

"Gartenlieder," for mixed chorus a capella, Op. 3. Furore, Kassel, 1988.

Secular a capella choruses of 1846 (vols. 1-5): *"Im Wald," Op. 3, No. 6; "Lockung," Op. 3. No. 1; "Abendlich," Op.3, No. 5; "Waldeinsam," "Morgendämmerung," "Seid gegrüsst," Op. 3, No. 3; "Komm," "Ariel," "Schweight der Menschen laute Lust," "Morgengruss," Op. 3, No. 4; "Schöne Fremde," Op. 3, No. 2; "Schweigend sinkt die Nacht hernieder," "Lust'ge Vögel," "O Herbst," "Schon kehren die Vögel wieder, ein," "Wer will mir wehren zu singen."*
Furore Kassel, 1988.

Works for soloists, chorus and orchestra.

Hiob (Job), cantata for soloists, chorus and orchestra. Conrad Misch, ed.
Furore, Kassel, 1992.

Io d'amor, o Dio, Io moro, concert aria for soprano and orchestra.
Bote & Bock, Berlin, 1992.

Lobgesang, cantata for soloists, chorus and orchestra.
Conrad Misch, ed. Furore, Kassel, 1992.

9. Clara Wieck, from an 1835 lithograph

10. Clara Schumann

MADAME SCHUMANN.

11. Robert Schumann, lithograph
by Josef Kriehuber, in 1839.

Chapter 3

Clara Schumann

1819 - 1896

"There is no greater joy than composing something oneself and then listening to it. – There are some nice passages in the Trio And I believe it is also fairly successful as far as form is concerned but naturally it is still women's work which always lacks force and occasionally invention."

Clara Schumann 1853

The Trio referred to is *Opus 17 for Piano, Violin and Cello,* considered, by many, to be her most outstanding work.

Although being born only 14 years after Fanny Mendelssohn, Clara outlived her by nearly 50 years. Even though she was a woman she was able to travel widely and play in concerts throughout Europe. She journeyed as far as Britain and Russia, built a career that spanned 60 years and earned international acclaim as a renowned pianist.

Despite her confidence as a performer she had great inner conflicts about the worthiness of her skill as a composer. She persevered whilst Robert, her husband was alive to encourage her, but after he died in 1856 she wrote only one work choosing, instead, to edit and promote his music in preference to her own.

Clara's early life was not dissimilar to that of Maria Mozart and Fanny Mendelssohn. She received excellent musical tuition at home but this was purely because her father, realising her great ability, intended her to have a great artistic career as a professional musician. It was not, as was the case for most young women, because musical prowess was considered an asset in the marriage market.

There were three stages in the progress of her life; the first 20 years when she lived under the supervision of her father; 16 years when she was married to Robert Schumann, and the 40 years left to her after his death when she found herself breadwinner to their large family. During these latter years she used her talent to build up a career as a performer and teacher, on a par with men, and so doing earned a living, great honour and the respect of many male composers, who readily allowed her to perform their works.

Her music was her fulfilment. She was at her happiest when at the piano, yet her life was one of obligation, firstly to her father in his desire to make her into a brilliant young pianist; secondly in support of her husband, Robert, during his tragically disturbing mental illnesses and finally, left with seven children, her need to earn money to support them.

Clara Josephine Wieck was born in Leipzig, on September 30th, 1819, the second of five children. Her father was Friedrich Wieck (1785-1873), her mother Marianne Tromlitz (1797-1872). Their eldest daughter Adelheid, born in 1817, died when she was only nine months old. After Clara, Marianne gave birth to three boys, Alwin in 1821, Gustav in 1823 and Victor in 1824.

Three months after Victor's birth Marianne left Friedrich, and returned to her father's home in Plauen, with Clara, who was nearly five, and the baby, Victor, who died before he was three. The other two boys remained with their father.

When Clara reached the age of five Friedrich demanded that she be returned to him. According to Saxon law children were legally the property of their father.

A divorce was granted to the Wiecks on January 22nd, 1825. Within a few months Marianne married Adolph Bargiel, a music teacher whom Friedrich had worked with when he had been private tutor to the children of Baron von Seckendorff in Querfurth. Bargiel had become a family friend and the growing relationship between Adolph and Marianne had been a contributory factor in the breakup of the Wieck's marriage.

Marianne was distraught at losing her children. Friedrich allowed her to see them while she still lived in Leipzig, but after the Bargiels moved to Berlin, where Adolph took over a piano school, the Logier Institute, this contact became less frequent.

Friedrich Wieck was a self-trained musician and extremely ambitious. He was as demanding and obsessive as were the fathers of Nannerl and Fanny, compelling first his wife, Marianne, and then his daughter Clara to work ceaselessly to create musical careers in order to build up his own prestige.

He was born in 1785 in Pretzsch, a small town about 45 kilometers from Leipzig. His father was a merchant but unsuccessful, and although Friedrich showed obvious musical talent, the family were poor. His schooldays were haphazard due to his own poor health and his musical education minimal. However he did, eventually, attend the University of Wittenburg to study Theology, graduated and became a private tutor, a role taken by university graduates who had neither money nor connections.

As a teacher he was conscientious, observant and had an enquiring mind. His desire to be a musician never diminished. He became self-taught, learning to play the piano and acquiring enough theory to compose. In 1815 he sent some songs to the composer Carl Maria Von Weber who was gracious enough to write a detailed criticism of them. The songs were published and reviewed in a Leipzig journal, the *Allgemeine Musikalische Zeitung,* the critic noting that they showed *"some indications of talent."*

As a result of this, and with some financial backing from a friend, Friedrich, at the age of 30, gave up his role as tutor and set up as a piano teacher and owner of a music shop.

On June 23rd 1816 he married Marianne who was one of his students. This marriage was advantageous for him in musical circles. Marianne's father was the Cantor in Plauen, her grandfather a leading flautist and flutemaker.

Marianne was 19 and highly gifted as a singer and pianist. The marriage lasted for only eight years during which time she sang solos at the weekly concerts in the Leipzig Gewandhaus, helped in the business, entertained guests, ran the household, gave singing and piano lessons, practiced for her performances and gave birth to five children.

As for Friedrich his reputation grew through her talents, as did his prestige every time she performed.

It is evident that life was very hard for Marianne during the years of her marriage. She had met Friedrich in his role as a piano teacher, a position in which he had acquired a good reputation for his skills, intelligence and talent. At the age of 19 she may have been impressed by his obvious success but unprepared for his insensitivity in his demands on her and for his cruel temper.

She was, however, a tough and independent young woman, a necessary quality that helped her to make the decision to leave him and return to her father. It was rare for a married couple to be divorced as this cast a slur on a woman's reputation.

Adolph Bargiel, whom she then married, was completely different in his attitude towards her. He was gentle and loving, better educated, musically, than Friedrich but lacked business acumen. Friedrich considered him to be weak and sickly.

Unfortunately the Logier Institute, in which Adolph taught piano in Berlin, closed in 1830, due to a cholera epidemic. Soon afterwards he suffered a stroke from which he never really recovered, and in 1841 he died.

Marianne, left with their four children, was forced to give piano lessons in order to support them. Woldemar Bargiel, one of her sons from this second marriage, became a composer and conductor and a close friend of his half sister Clara.

Clara did not speak until she was over four years old. Her father was domineering and cruel, physically abusing Gustav and Alwin. He raged at her mother if she did not live up to his onerous expectations. She was expected to be artist, teacher and homemaker, and it was more comfortable for Clara to shut herself away from this unpleasant battleground and exist in a world of silence.

It wasn't surprising that she turned to music. Pianos were played constantly, by her mother rehearsing, by students taught by her father and by customers trying out instruments in the shop. To Clara music seemed safe. It was not angry or threatening and listening to it gave her great joy.

Even though her parents thought she was deaf and seemingly dull witted she began to reproduce tunes at the piano that she had heard, and her father, realising that her interest might be the beginnings of a seed to be nurtured, began to teach her some simple pieces by ear. To his great delight she learned and remembered them without difficulty.

It was when she returned from her short spell with her mother that Friedrich began to give her formal piano lessons with two other girls of a similar age. It is possible that this interaction with other children began to stimulate her speech and it wasn't long before she spoke in full sentences. However her apparent deafness lingered until she was almost eight.

"On 18 September (1824) my father actually began to teach me the piano. I had easily learned some exercises – before I went with my mother to Plauen, and I had played by ear some easy accompaniments for dancing."

These words of Clara's were written in her diary, by her father, who wrote in her name until 1831, after which Friedrich allowed Clara to write some entries herself, if she had time, and, of course, he made sure she had very little.

For four years Clara lived a motherless life, with her brothers, under the care of her father and their servants. Friedrich had excitedly come to the realisation that she showed all the signs of becoming a child prodigy, and because of this she received his undivided attention. Her brothers, who did not have her musical aptitude, were practically ignored.

By the time she reached seven she worked at the piano for three hours each day. Her general education was meagre. For a year and a half she attended school but after that tutors were engaged to teach her French and English, two languages that her father deemed essential for her future international career.

Her health and physical development were also important and, as part of the daily routine, the household went for long walks that lasted for several hours. Clara joined in these walks from the age of three, and this was to become a routine that she kept up throughout her life, attributing her good health to this regular exercise.

She had a wide-ranging musical education. The Cantor at St. Thomas' Church, Christian Theodor Weinlig taught her theory and counterpoint and the Director of the Leipzig Opera, Heinrich Dorn, gave her lessons in composition. Later, when they toured, Friedrich engaged tutors in a variety of venues, to continue her musical education, including orchestration, singing and violin playing.

There was not much time for reading or other childish activities. Friedrich's intention was to make her into a virtuoso and from the age of six took her to operas and concerts at the Gewandhaus so that she heard and saw the best performers of the time. By the time she was 12 she had seen operas by Mozart, Beethoven, Weber and Rossini, and dramas written by Lessing, Goethe and Schiller.

In 1829 she began teaching her brother Alwin to play the piano. He was two years her junior. Her father believed that this would be a useful learning process for her as most performers added to their reputation and income by teaching students.

The musical life of Leipzig was active and established and had one of the first music colleges in Germany. The citizens took pride in their church music, university, and unique Gewandhaus concerts, in which Clara was to play more frequently than any other performer. Friedrich became very well respected in the musical life of the city. He was known as a sound businessman and sought after teacher. His house in Grimmaische Strasse was an open door to visiting composers and performers.

Thus Leipzig attracted the talents of many visiting musicians, one of whom was Niccolo Paganini. When Friedrich heard that he was to play in a series of concerts he took Clara to meet him. She played a duet, with her father and one of her own compositions,

Polonaise in E flat major. Friedrich intended to show that Clara was receiving excellent tuition and had a great talent for the piano, and that he encouraged her to compose knowing that a virtuoso's career involved performing their own compositions as well as those by other composers. Paganini was suitably impressed saying that she *"had an artistic career ahead of her, since she had sensitivity."*

Encouraged by Paganini's comments Friedrich arranged concerts at home in which Clara was able to perform. She was also invited to play at other private gatherings. Dr. Ernst Carus, director of a mental hospital at Colditz Castle, and ardent music lover, hosted one such occasion. Clara played the *Trio Op. 96* by Hummel, with professional musicians and was quoted as being *"less deficient than the gentlemen that accompanied her."* She was then only nine years old.

Another visitor to this musical evening was Robert Schumann, nine years her senior. He was also a gifted pianist and so impressed by Clara's playing that he begged permission from his mother to give up law and study music. He became a student of Friedrich's for about a year, and boarder in the Wieck household until Clara and her father left on a concert tour to Paris.

When she was nine, in 1828, Friedrich remarried. His new wife was Clementine Fechner, aged 23, daughter of a pastor Samuel Traugott Fechner. She was a welcome addition to the two young motherless boys, but as far as Clara was concerned was a rival to her father's attentions. Clara had become used to being the *"star"* of the family. Her father's whole existence was centred around her. She had her own room. He bought her special pianos from Vienna, and silk gowns to wear for her concerts.

How fortunate it was that Clementine accepted the situation into which she had married. She was intelligent and cultured but not a musician. She managed the household and piano business very capably when her husband and Clara were on tours, handled his correspondence and brought obedience and great patience to a marriage that lasted for 45 years.

The relationship between Clementine and her new stepdaughter was always strained and Clara's lively nature that she controlled in her father's presence was often exhibited in an ill-tempered fashion towards her stepmother.

Friedrich and Clementine had three children but only one, Marie, born in 1832, survived.

Marie was educated along the same path as Clara, had a fairly successful career as a pianist but never rose to the heights of fame achieved by her elder half-sister. She worshipped her father but towards Clara she was hostile and jealous.

Clara's first solo concert took place at the Gewandhaus on November 8th 1830 and the reviews were everything that Friedrich could wish for.

" – the eleven-year-old daughter of a local piano dealer and expert piano teacher – earned her the greatest applause."

This success was a spur for Friedrich and he immediately plunged into arranging Clara's first tour to Paris. It did not seem to matter to him that he was leaving his wife, who was pregnant, his other children, his business and his students, to devote himself to his daughter's future career.

They left Leipzig in September 1831 and did not return until the following May. On their journey they stayed in many towns, including Weimar and Frankfurt where Clara played in private homes as well as concert halls. They reached their final destination, Paris on the 15th February 1832.

In Weimar they met the poet Goethe who, on hearing Clara play rewarded her with a medal and his portrait inscribed, *"For the gifted artist Clara Wieck."*

Friedrich was determined that Clara's performances received good publicity and contacted Robert Schumann, who had become involved in musical journalism in Leipzig. The result of this was a review in the *Allgemeine musikalische Zeitung,*

"The artist who is still so young reaped thundering approval – indeed, the great skill, assurance, and strength with which she plays even the most difficult movements so easily is highly remarkable."

Moving from place to place enforced an enormous amount of organisation, and four months spent staying in small towns caused innumerable problems. Friedrich had to search for lodgings, rent concert halls, find good pianos, obtain suitable food, make useful contacts, publicize the event, interest knowledgeable audiences and hopefully collect plenty of money. Many of these elements were difficult to accomplish and caused him much annoyance.

However, this first hand experience was a great learning process for Clara forming a basis for the time, years later, when she had to organise her own tours.

Whilst in Frankfurt, they learnt that Clementine had given birth to Marie, in January 1832. This was obviously a momentous occasion for the young mother but perhaps not quite so for Friedrich, who had fathered five children already. He did, however, write affectionately to his wife asking briefly about her welfare and that of the new baby, but then spent the remainder of the letter describing in great detail Clara's recent concert success.

Although Friedrich felt the strain of travelling, Clara seemed to flourish, receiving glowing notices in each town, and every day managed to find the time to go for walks, practice the piano, work on compositions and study new works by other composers.

When they eventually arrived in Paris Eduard Fechner, Clementine's brother, who was a painter, met them. He proved invaluable to Friedrich, who found the French language difficult. Fechner was able to organise their accommodation, invitations to soirées, mentions in newspapers and inclusion in concerts.

It was at soirées that aspiring players sought recognition for their talents. They were held in the stately homes of aristocrats or wealthy music lovers. Clara, as a young girl, had to dress entirely in white and have a new dress for each appearance. At the age of 12 she found the hours that these events were held extremely difficult as they did not begin until 10 at night and continued on until one in the morning.

The Paris visit did not fulfil all Friedrich's hopes. He was disappointed when a concert by Paganini, in which Clara was to be a supporting artist, was cancelled due to the maestro's ill health. Also a cholera outbreak forced another concert to be rescheduled which was very badly attended.

They did, however, make many useful contacts, notable musicians including Hiller, Chopin, Liszt and Mendelssohn who became future colleagues and lifelong friends.

Friedrich never forgot the poverty of his childhood and his longing for money was well known in Leipzig. Schumann referred to him as *"Meister Allesgeld,"* (Master-all-for-money).

He was often to be found standing at the door collecting payment from concertgoers. He peddled engravings of Clara's portrait painted by Fechner; despised gifts of jewellery turning it immediately into cash, and bartered for French and theory lessons for Clara by offering the loan of a guitar or piano from his shop.

Clara was rewarded with a little money and occasional jewellery. These were logged down as expenses, the rest Friedrich invested in state bonds.

It wasn't until 1839 when Clara wished to marry Robert, against her father's wishes, that she realised his exploitation. Friedrich refused to give her any of the money that she had earned, stating that he was entitled to them, and as a woman, she was still bound by social and economic restrictions that allowed him full control of her money. He also stated that he had neglected his other children, his business and his pupils to devote himself totally to her artistic career and thus had a moral right to it.

It was only after she had left him to marry Robert that the matter was settled in court, but the damage had been done. Friedrich, through his own unbending dominance had caused a rift between the two of them that took many years to overcome and caused Clara, at the age of 21, to become completely dependant on her new husband, and controller of her own musical future.

Robert and Clara's relationship blossomed during her teenage years. It was only when Robert first moved in as a student that she and her brothers enjoyed any childhood activities. During the day they worked and practiced together but in the evenings he would take her to his room, with her brothers, where he would entertain them by playing charades and games, and stimulate, sometimes frighten their receptive minds, with imaginative stories.

It wasn't surprising that the serious young girl, who knew

nothing other than a structured musical life, should come to love the good looking young man with long brown hair and deep expressive blue eyes.

As for Robert he saw a pretty face with a slightly pointed chin and enormous strangely angled eyes, and a mouth that at times bore a wistful expression that momentarily showed her childhood unhappiness.

She was never subjected to the violence that her father wreaked on his sons, probably because she had potential moneymaking abilities, but she did suffer verbal abuse. Friedrich often told her that she was *"lazy and stubborn,"* and to a child who loved playing the piano, withheld lessons and favourite pieces, as punishment.

However the docile daughter started to grow up. Robert noting this wrote, *"Clara displays great obstinacy toward her stepmother, who is certainly a woman worthy of respect. The old man rebukes Clara, but nevertheless he is coming under her thumb more and more. She is giving orders like a senora."*

As the tours continued Clara's defiance of her father grew. When she was 15, in 1834, they visited Magdeburg, Hannover and other northern cities. On this tour Friedrich found her to be a rebellious adolescent."

"Clara now is often so inconsiderate, domineering, full of unreasonable opposition, careless, totally disobedient, rude, prickly, blunt, monstrously lazy, capriciously vain - "

It was obvious that he felt his dominance over her threatened. She had been the apple of his eye and earner of a sizeable income that gave him status and prestige. He had enjoyed the largesse of rich noblemen, mingled with eminent musicians and had enjoyed the kudos and applause of his daughter's success. But it was obvious that her growing sexuality was attracting a host of young men, including Robert Schumann, in whom she showed signs of great interest.

Robert Alexander Schumann was born on 8th June 1810 in Zwickau, a town about 40 miles from Leipzig. He was the youngest (and a late) son of August Schumann, a publisher, bookseller and writer, and Johanne Christiane Schnabel, daughter of a surgeon. He had three older brothers, Eduard, Julius and Carl.

Robert showed musical talent at a very early age was encouraged by his parents and taught by a local music teacher, Johann Gottfried Kuntsch.

When he was 16 his father died and Gottlob Rudel, a friend of the family and local merchant became his guardian.

He graduated from the Zwickau Lyceum, where he had been an outstanding student and travelled to Leipzig to enrol at the university, supposedly to study law. But this was just a cover up. His real interests lay in music and literature. He rarely attended lectures but spent his time playing the piano, composing, and reading. He fell in love with every pretty woman that he met, drank heavily, smoked and was always short of money.

He moved to Heidelberg to continue his law studies, travelled to Italy and, when he returned, finally made up his mind. He would change his career from Law to Music.

It seemed as if meeting the Wiecks at the house of Dr. Carus had triggered this decision and he wrote a letter to his mother asking for her support.

"My entire life has been a twenty-year struggle between poetry and prose, or if you like, call it music and the law – Now I am standing at the crossroads, and the question "Which way?" frightens me. If I follow my guardian angel, he points to art, and, I believe, to the right way."

His mother agreed, after writing to Friedrich for his opinion. She was a typically worried parent, aware that her talented son had virtually wasted three years at university and squandered a large amount of money in doing so.

Friedrich's response laid down many rules for lessons and practicing, boasted about his achievements, informed her of Clara's success so young, and finally, rather condescendingly, assured Frau Schumann that he could turn her son into *"one of the greatest pianists now living."*

Thus the matter was settled and Robert, as mentioned earlier, moved into the Wieck household, as a lodger and pupil.

It is surprising how readily Friedrich agreed to this arrangement, but it seems that whatever objections he had, years later, concerning Robert as Clara's suitor, he did, in fact, appreciate and value that the young man had great gifts as a performer and composer.

But life was not easy for Robert in this environment. There was always friction between tutor and student. Although he greatly admired Friedrich's teaching skills, he battled against doing some of the physical exercises and training that his piano instruction required. Also, although admiring Clara's youthful talent he disliked Friedrich's attitude of comparing his ability with hers. Even so, during this time, the relationship between Robert and Clara blossomed, growing from respect, friendship to love.

Sometime during the year spent in the Wieck household Robert injured his hand. This may have been due to the strengthening exercises imposed on him by Friedrich, but the result caused him great despondency and the realisation that he could not continue as an aspiring pianist.

Finally accepting the situation he decided to put all his efforts into his compositions, chiefly because he had Clara who could ably perform them. When he heard her play his second published work, *"Papillons,"* he wrote, *"I have never yet heard Clara play as she did today – everything was played masterfully and also beautifully."*

Alongside his composing Robert worked as a journalist, eventually becoming owner and editor of the Neue Zeitschrift für Musik.

Even though Clara and her father spent months away on tour, and Robert became involved with several other young women, their involvement continued, and in November 1835, when Clara was 16, they had their first kiss. Clara's happiness was expressed in a letter written to him later, *"When you gave me that first kiss, I thought I would faint; everything went blank and I could barely hold the lamp that was lighting your way out."*

Naively Robert believed that Friedrich would welcome him as a husband for Clara, but in this respect, he was completely wrong. He had underestimated the possessiveness of a father who saw their romance as a clandestine affair and also his domination over his talented daughter, threatened.

Their courtship was of necessity built on covert meetings and undisclosed letters. They became secretly engaged on August 14th 1837, and Robert wrote in his diary, *"It is a union for eternity."* However when he approached Friedrich on 13th, September, Clara's 18th birthday, and formally asked for her hand in marriage, he was refused. In his humiliation Robert wrote, *"This coldness, this ill will, this confusion, these contradictions – he has a new way to destroy, he thrusts blade and hilt into my heart."*

Clara knew that if she wanted to be with Robert she must break away from her father. Their final tour to Vienna in 1837 proved to be an outstanding success. It was also Friedrich's greatest financial triumph. He wrote to his wife, *"All Vienna is saying that no artist has ever made a sensation like this – now the whole world shall know there is only one Clara, a Clara at whose feet all Vienna lies."*

On March 15th, 1838 Clara was awarded the greatest distinction that Austria could give. She was named *Konigliche Kaiserliche Kammervirtuosin (Royal and Imperial Chamber Virtuosa)*. Musicians and royalty honoured her, and publishers fought to publish her works.

But Friedrich's health was suffering. He had found the organisation of this latest tour, along with Clara's contrariness, tough to handle yet he still remained adamant in his refusal to allow her to marry Robert.

Thus the affair went to court and consent was granted to their marriage. Many of Friedrich's acquaintances were appalled at his attitude towards the young lovers. Robert was an intellectual with obvious genius, had inherited a small legacy, was developing as a composer and ran a successful music journal. There seemed no reason for his refusal apart from the loss of Clara as a financial asset. All his arguments centred on the fact that he did not believe that Robert was financially stable, and that marriage would mean the end of Clara's career.

But he had underestimated his daughter's tenacity. Clara

began to arrange her own tours, made some good and lasting friendships especially with Henriette Reichmann, Emilie List and Pauline Garcia and gained the respect of many eminent musicians including Meyerbeer and Berlioz. Much to his annoyance Friedrich realised that she could do very well without him.

Yet, however badly he behaved towards Clara, Robert had to face the fact that she was greatly attached to her father. He had been the inspiration of her musical life, had built her career and because of this she found parting from him difficult.

She wrote to Robert, *" I am his daughter, and though I feel bitter at times, yet I still love Father so much. – He loves me too much to push me away from him forever. Be calm, my Robert, he loves you too; he just will not admit it."*

Clara was now spending most of her time on tour or staying with friends. From September 1839 she lived with her mother. Her father forbade her to return home, withheld her possessions and kept all her money for himself.

She was greatly upset by the poverty of the Bargiel's and felt that her presence was an added burden. She saw how difficult her mother's life was, nursing a sick husband, caring for her children and giving piano lessons to earn a living.

As Clara was practically penniless, Robert cashed in some of his state bonds. With these and her current earnings she was able to pay her way and help the family.

But the stress was beginning to tell on her especially as Robert was experiencing anxiety attacks and depression because of the court case. The strain manifested itself in pain in her fingers, fainting spells and neuralgia. *"I have a great number of worries. – I seem so weak at the piano – it is enough to make me despair."* She had to draw on every ounce of her stamina and energy to get through this difficult time.

But when the court case was decided in their favour, Clara and Robert were married on September 12th 1840 and moved into their first home together, an apartment on Inselstrasse in Leipzig.

Clara did not adapt easily to her new role as a wife, realising that Robert expected her to run their home rather than be a performer and composer. She found this change disturbing and was conscious of having to curb her energy and talents. She had always had access to a piano, to practice and compose but now found that she had to concede its use to Robert, and could only play when he was out.

This was demoralising, as she was, after all, a famous pianist who had written and performed her own works. She had never had to share with another, and this, along with the everyday tasks of a married woman, was very difficult to accept.

However her days were always filled. Almost every musician visiting Leipzig called on them during the first year of their marriage, including Mendelssohn, and William Sterndale Bennett, as well as old friends, poets and publishers.

Robert expected that his work should take precedence over Clara's. He did, however, encourage her to keep composing, when she could, and was pleased to receive three songs at Christmas that she had written especially for him.

Clara persevered, with the time she was allowed, and was determined to make her debut as a married woman. This she did at a Gewandhaus concert on March 31st 1841. It was conducted by Mendelssohn and contained the first performance of Robert's *Spring Symphony, Op. 38*. Clara played one of her own songs *Am Strand* (On the shore) and also works by Chopin, Mendelssohn and Thalberg.

Robert called it *"an unforgettable evening – My Clara played everything like a master and in such an inspired mood that everyone was enchanted."*

A year after they were married Clara gave birth to a daughter, Marie on September 1st 1841. The birth of this first daughter gave her great joy and she was always her best-loved child. Marie never married but later devoted her life to her mother's career. She became teacher, secretary, seamstress and child carer and took charge of their home when her mother was on tour.

Clara conceived easily and over the next 13 years gave birth to seven more children.

Her second daughter Elise, born in 1843 was the most independent of their children. Elise left home to become a governess, married and lived for six years in the United States before returning to Germany.

Julie, born in 1845 was delicate and had fragile health. She married an Italian Count, but died in 1872 from tuberculosis.

Emil, born in 1846 was their first son, and also suffered from bad health. He died when only 16 months old.

Ludwig probably caused his mother the most anguish. He was born in 1848 and always exhibited a strange personality. He entered a mental hospital at the age of 22, was diagnosed with a spinal disease that affected his brain and died there in 1899, three years after the death of his mother.

Ferdinand, born in 1849, was called up to fight in the Franco-Prussian War of 1870, survived but developed rheumatism, became an addict due to being treated with morphine, and died from its affects, aged 42. He left a widow and six children for whom Clara had to give financial support.

Eugenie, the youngest daughter was born in 1851. She never knew her father and spent her childhood at a boarding school. She had considerable musical talent, became a teacher and performer and spent 20 years in England. Although, as a child she saw little of her mother she wrote, in her memoirs, *"But one thing I know for certain, that wherever she might be, we were ever conscious of her loving care, - and to us little ones, - she was the greatest thing we possessed in the world."*

Felix, born in 1854, was the most gifted of the Schumann children, both in music and literature, but also suffered from tuberculosis and died in 1879, aged 24.

Robert may have assumed that having children would put a halt to his wife's concert performances but in this he was completely wrong. Clara did not allow motherhood to tie her down. She boarded her babies with relatives, hired wet nurses and nursemaids and happily went off on tours. Between 1840 and 1854, when she was nearly always pregnant, she gave 139 concerts.

She was always conscious of rivals. The up and coming

performer of the moment was, Anton Rubinstein who, at the age of 12 was already setting out on an illustrious career.

To Robert, Clara's continuing career stimulated a crisis. A woman, even though married, could not travel alone, so he had to accompany her. Clara's natural robustness coped with home, children, pregnancies, travelling and performing without any trouble, but Robert was often ill, physically and mentally. He suffered from vertigo and faintness, was diagnosed with *"nerve fever"* and at one point believed he was going blind.

As Robert's illnesses and depressions grew more frequent Clara compensated by taking on extra work. She did not initially face up to fact that he had a serious problem. Money was always of paramount importance and even though Robert earned steadily with his composing and editing, Clara knew that she could make more in a three-week tour than he could in a year. She did not realise for a moment that this was a blow to his pride.

In 1844 Robert gave up, with reluctance, the editorship of the *Neue Zeitschrift*, passing it on to Oswald Lorenz. He had built up the journal over a period of ten years to the position whereby it had achieved an international reputation and become financially successful. However, he felt that he needed to simplify his life and concentrate more on his own composing.

Later in 1844 the family moved to Dresden. The reason for this was mainly because of Robert's health. Dresden was situated on the Elbe and surrounded by hills. The air was purer as there was little industry to pollute it.

Also Friedrich lived there. Recently there had been an attempt at reconciliation between them and Clara, optimistically, hoped for his support.

The Dresden years were productive for Robert. Many of his best-known works were written there but for Clara her career, out of necessity, had slowed down. Robert's health along with a string of pregnancies and her obligations as a wife meant that her concerts were limited to the near vicinity, but even so they provided her with a considerable income which she and Robert added to by giving lessons in piano and composition.

One of the notable incidents of the Dresden years took place during the May uprising of 1849. Robert sympathised with the rebels who expected every man fit enough to fight for them. Clara realised that Robert was not well enough and hid him for as long as she could. Eventually they managed to escape to safety with Marie, leaving the other children behind. It is said that Clara courageously returned to fetch them, walking through the embattled city, even though she was seven months pregnant.

Robert began to rely on her not only as a wife but also as a musician. She used her expert training to arrange his music, served as assistant conductor and accompanist for his choral group, coached at rehearsals and premiered all his great piano works. Other musicians noted this close partnership with admiration. Marie von Lindemann, a singer in the choral society wrote, *"With what calm, with what confidence he turned to his Clara --- and how we saw her eyes flash with enthusiasm when the beauty of his music was appreciated."*

Clara's career took second place during the Dresden years, as Robert's became more successful. By 1849 his works were eagerly sought after by publishers.

But the reconciliation between Friedrich and Clara was short-lived. She became greatly upset by his arrogance. He would not acknowledge Robert's success and forbade his best students to sing in his choral works. Thus Friedrich was cold-shouldered. He was not invited to the premieres of Robert's current works whereas Marianne, Clara's mother, became a frequent and welcome visitor to their house.

Clara became Robert's protector. He became totally dependant on her. She took over many of his responsibilities. Though he would have preferred her to be mother and wife, he took pride in her talents. He wrote to Mendelssohn, *"She is a gift from above – there is no doubt that she really deserves affection and encouragement as an industrious and hardworking artist, and indeed as a woman too."*

Yet there were limits to Clara's stamina. In 1847 after having played in tours to Berlin and Vienna, performed in a Schumann

Festival in Zwickau, suffered the death of Emil, realised that she was once again pregnant, she wrote in her diary, *"I am lazy, but I cannot help it because I am always ill and terribly weak. Oh, if I could only work, that is my one sorrow."*

In September 1850 they moved to Düsseldorf. Robert had been appointed Music Director of the Municipal Orchestra and Chorus. Their reputation had instigated this move and initially they were treated with great respect. However within a year there was dissatisfaction with Robert's work.

His conducting style was criticised as was his handling of discipline within the choir and he often failed to turn up for rehearsals. Clara supported him loyally although she realised that his mental illness was getting worse.

She, however, was in great demand, playing in concerts in Holland, Leipzig and Hanover and a great many students came from all over Germany to study with her.

In January 1853 they moved into a new apartment where Clara had her own piano and could practice and compose without disturbing Robert. It was here that she wrote her last pieces including *Variations on a theme of Robert Schumann, and six songs –Opus 20 – 23.*

The attitude of the choir and musicians towards Robert manifested in a lessening of his involvement. He was only asked to conduct his own works. Clara reacted as any wife would, *"I cannot say how angry I was and how bitter it was for me not to be able to spare Robert this outrage."*

But Robert's symptoms caused him to become withdrawn. He had mild strokes, was lacking in stamina and suffered from auditory hallucinations.

In February 1854 the final breakdown came. His headaches and mood swings grew worse and on the 27th he attempted suicide. For his own safety and that of his family he was taken to a sanatorium in Endenich, a suburb of Bonn. Clara was forbidden to visit him as his mental health was so fragile, but later they did exchange letters.

Robert remained in the sanatorium for two and a half years. Clara received weekly reports but was unable to visit him until two days before his death. She wrote, *"The pain, the longing for him, just to have one more glance from him, to let him feel that I am near – he looked at me so lovingly, embraced me once again – this comforting memory will never leave me."*

After his death on 29th July 1856 her sorrow was reflected in these words, *"God give me strength to live without him. All my happiness was taken with his death."*

At the age of 37, Clara found herself a widow with seven children to support. Marie, the eldest was 15, and the youngest, Felix, only two, having been born four months after his father had entered the sanatorium.

After the terrible days following Robert's hospitalisation Clara had turned to her friends and family for support especially her mother, the violinist Joseph Joachim and composer Johannes Brahms.

Joachim had introduced Clara and Robert to Brahms in 1853. Even though he was only 20 years old, he had already become an accomplished pianist and composer. His compositions immediately impressed them, and his expressive eyes, long fair hair and interesting face.

Robert had always given generously of his time to advise and assist other composers. Clara wrote of Brahms, in her diary, *"Robert loves him and takes great pleasure in him, both the man and the artist."* She too was swept along with his freshness and enthusiasm.

During the period of Robert's illness Brahms lived in an apartment nearby and helped daily with the children, even keeping the household books. It was as if he had stepped into the shoes of a husband.

Whether Brahms had hopes of marrying Clara, even though she was 14 years older, has been widely speculated. There was an undoubted love between them. His music gave her great joy. She sought his advice and opinion on her own playing, depended on his support in all the decisions that she made concerning tours and teaching positions, and involved him as a surrogate father in the lives of her children.

However Clara did not marry again. Her main priority, for the rest of her life, was to earn enough money to support her large family.

Brahms also avoided matrimony even though he met and admired many suitable young women. Clara was often unhappy when he showed an interest in ladies younger than her, especially when one of them was her own daughter, Julie. It was a relief when Julie chose to marry Count Marmorito in September 1869.

The only help Clara accepted, financially, was a loan from Paul Mendelssohn, the banker, and this she insisted on paying back as speedily as she could. It was due to her inherent determination and hard work that she built up a successful career as a performer, during the 40 years following her husband's death.

Towards the end of 1856 she wrote her last piece of music, *Romance in B minor*, in memory of Robert. She missed his input in her writing, the boost he had always given her when her confidence was low, and realising that her strengths lay in performing she felt she would achieve more as an interpreter of piano works than as a composer.

To this end she arranged her professional life in order to support her family. Her engagements often meant travelling for ten months of the year, but even so the well being of her children was undertaken meticulously by mail, to housekeepers, governesses, boarding schools and relatives.

As for the children they grew up knowing that they would rarely see her. She was seldom with them for birthdays, confirmations or holidays and when they were ill she was not there to comfort them.

They were, however, given the best musical education that she could afford, at the same time being discouraged from becoming professional musicians. It might be assumed that having a famous name would be an advantage, but it was this very name that caused Clara to dissuade them. Felix, especially was eager for a musical career but he was persuaded, until his early death, to follow the path of three of his sisters and teach rather than perform.

In 1857 Clara moved the family from Dusseldorff to an apartment in Berlin, but this did not satisfy her needs and in 1862 she bought a house in Baden-Baden that was a base for them for ten years. The spa, lake and mountains provided a restful haven for Clara when she returned from her tours.

They called it the *"dog kennel"* but with its salon, five downstairs rooms, two kitchens and plenty of bedrooms Clara considered it big enough, *"for all the children to be together with me in the summer."*

But this hopeful relaxation was overshadowed by considerable worries about them. Ludwig was diagnosed with an incurable brain disease in 1870 resulting in his committal to an asylum. Felix developed a serious lung condition and Julie had to be sent to a spa because of her weak health. Ferdinand, who had developed severe rheumatism due to having served in the Franco-Prussian war, had been prescribed morphine that gradually destroyed him, and at this period of Clara's life, when she wanted her children around her, Elise left home to become a teacher in Frankfurt.

Even though she charged high fees for concerts the expenses caused by her children's illnesses were a great drain on her finances, and although many people thought her well off, they were mistaken in their belief. Twice she was burgled losing jewellery and valuable mementoes given to her by wealthy patrons. Only her closest friends knew how she struggled to make ends meet.

Added to these family problems came the death of her mother and daughter Julie in 1872, and her father, the following year.

In 1873 she sold the house in Baden-Baden and moved to Berlin. She was forced to slow down her playing due to pains in her arms. Because of this, her debts began to rise, incurred mostly by the medical costs of her three sons. Fortunately royalties from performances, published editions of Robert's music and gifts from foundations became available at that time and brought an added boost to her dwindling income.

There were highlights, however, during that year, one of which was her appearance at the Bonn Music Festival where she played Robert's Piano Concerto in the presence of all her surviving children and many close friends including Jenny Lind, Brahms, Joachim and Hiller.

Clara did not settle happily to the lessening of her concert life. In a letter to Brahms in 1874 she wrote, *"I get so melancholy when I cannot be active. I have no talent for lazing about."*

She had always given piano lessons and decided, finally, in 1878, to take up a teaching position at the Hoch Conservatory in Frankfurt. She moved from Berlin buying herself a house on Myliusstrasse, where she settled for the remaining 18 years of her life.

It was a great achievement to become one of Clara's students. She was very selective, rigorously demanding and sometimes tactlessly direct in her criticism.

Yet she was greatly admired by both students and faculty members.

This was demonstrated, in a 50th Jubilee concert in her honour in 1878 when a complete programme of her music was performed. Then in Leipzig, the scene of her debut, aged 11, she was honoured by another concert, the programme consisting solely of music composed by Robert.

Ten years later in 1888, the tributes were overwhelming as her 60th anniversary arrived. Apart from concerts in her honour she received letters, flowers and poetry from all over the world. She wrote, *"I never suspected how much love was bestowed on me, and I am often quite embarrassed. --- The celebration brought many people closer to me, and I to them, and that is really gratifying."*

In these later years of her life she was an imposing and majestic figure, heavily built and always dressed in black, her silver hair covered with a lace veil. However it was her expressive eyes that were so captivating. They were large, yet gentle and seemed to change from grey to a silvery blue.

During the years since Robert's death the rheumatic attacks that she suffered in her arms, hands and fingers had caused her great distress. Concerts had been cancelled, she had been given opium, forced to rest her arm in a sling, and tried innumerable cures such as water treatment, electric shocks and massage.

Towards the end of her life she also developed gout, hearing problems and severe headaches. Her work had always been of paramount importance to her and she wrote, *"What is to happen to me if I can no longer play?"*

Her relationship with Brahms had remained lively and sometimes full of friction, yet they had built up a lifelong devotion to each other. In March 1891 it was his *Variations on a Theme by Haydn* that she played for her final public concert.

In the last two years of her life her melancholy grew. Only Marie remained at home. Felix had died in 1879 and Ferdinand in 1891. Ludwig remained in the asylum and eventually died three years after his mother.

Eugenie left to live in England in 1891, but Elise returned to Frankfurt, with her husband, after having lived in the USA, and gave support and comfort to her mother during her final years.

In March 1896 Clara lost her appetite and became emaciated. Having recovered from a slight stroke she then succumbed to a second, massive one and died on the 20th May 1896 at the age of 76. As she lay dying her grandson Ferdinand played Robert's *Intermezzi – Opus 4*, and the *F sharp major Romance – Opus 28*. This music, written by her beloved husband, was the last that she ever heard.

Brahms nearly missed her funeral, travelling to Frankfurt only to be told that it would take place in Bonn instead. Four days of memorial concerts followed her burial. He broke down in the middle of one of his performances and rushed out into the garden. On the last day he was in tears as he played his *Four Serious Songs*. These he later sent to Marie as a *"personal memorial for the death of your beloved mother."*

Brahms lived for less than a year after Clara, dying on 3rd April 1897.

Clara's life was spent in service to her family. She used her great talent to accomplish this, was able to spend her working life in an occupation that gave her the most pleasure, and a fulfilment that she could not live without.

But in her skills as a composer she had less confidence and gave up writing completely after the age of 36. She knew that, as a woman her compositions were not considered as acceptable as those written by men, and she resorted to the most lucrative way, for her, of earning a living, building on her great popularity as a concert pianist as well as editing and promoting her husband's work.

Today her compositions are becoming increasingly played and recorded. They include piano music, a piano trio and concerto, choral pieces and three Romances for violin and piano.

Clara Schumann was a woman among men, marching forward into the male dominated world, performing on a par with her male peers and gaining a reputation that was equal to theirs.

Published Works by Clara Schumann

With Opus Numbers – titles as they appear in first editions.

Op.1. *Quatre Polonoises pour le pianoforte. Published:*
Leipzig: Hofmeister, 1831

Op.2. *Caprices en forme de Valse pour le piano.*
Published: Paris: Stoepel ---Leipzig: Hofmeister, 1832.

Op.3. *Romance varie pour le piano*
Published: Leipzig: Hofmeister: --- Paris: Richault, 1833.

Op. 4. *Valses Romantiques pour le piano.*
Published: Leipzig: Whistling, 1835.
(None of the Instrumental parts have survived.)

Op. 5. *Quatre Pièces caractéristiques. No.1 Le Sabbat. No. 2. Caprice à la Boléro. No. 3. Romance. No. 4. Ballet des Revenants.*
Published: Leipzig: Whistling, 1835/36.

Op.6. *Soirées Musicales contenant Toccatina, Ballade, Nocturne, Polonaise et deux Mazurkas.*
Published: Leipzig: Hofmeister --- Paris: Richault, 1836.

Op. 7. *Premier Concert pour le Pianoforte avec accompagnement d'Orchestre.*
Published: Leipzig: Hofmeister --- Paris: Richault: ---Hamburg:
A Cranz, 1837.

Op. 8. *Variations de Concert pour le Pianoforte, sur la Cavatine du Pirate, de Bellini.*
Published: Vienna: Haslinger, 1837.

Op. 9. *Souvenir de Vienne. Impromptu.*
Published : Vienna: Diabelli, 1838.

Op.10. *Scherzo pour le Pianoforte.*
Published: Leipzig: Breitkopf & Härtel:--- Paris: Schonenberger, 1838.

Op.11. *Trois Romances pour le Piano.*
Published: Vienna; Mechetti; --- Paris: Richault, 1840

Op. 12. *Zwolf Gedichte aus F. Rückert's Liebesfrühling für Gesang und Pianoforte von Robert und Clara Schumann.* Three songs.
Published: Leipzig: Breithopf & Härtel, 1841

Op. 13. *Sechs Lieder mit Begleitung des Pianoforte*
Published: Leipzig: Breitkopf & Härtel, 1843.

Op. 14. *Deuxieme Scherzo pour le Pianoforte.*
Published: Leipzig: Breitkopf & Härtel, 1845.

Op. 15. *Quatre Pièces Fugitives pour le Pianoforte.*
Published: Leipzig: Breitkopf & Hartel, 1845.

Op. 16. *3 Praeludien und Fugen für das Pianoforte.*
Published: Leipzig: Breitkopf & Härtel, 1845.

Op. 17. *Trio für Pianoforte. Violine, und Violoncello.*
Published: Leipzig: Breitkopf & Härtel, 1847.

Op. 20. *Variationen für das Pianoforte über ein Thema von Robert Schumann.*
Published: Leipzig: Breitkopf & Härtel, 1854.

Op. 21. *Drei Romanzen für Pianoforte.*
Published: Leipzig: Breitkopf & Härtel, 1855/56.

Op. 22. *Drei Romanzen fur Pianoforte und Violine.*
Published: Leipzig: Breitkopf & Härtel, 1855/56.

Op. 23. *Sechs Lieder*
Published: Leipzig: Breitkopf & Härtel, 1855-1856

There are also published works without Opus numbers, unpublished works and other works mentioned in her diaries that are lost.

12. Nadezhda Nikolayevna Rimskaya-Korsakova

13. Portrait of Rimsky-Korsakov by Ilya Repin

Chapter 4

Nadezhda Rimsky-Korsakov

1848 - 1919

"Regarding the Symphony, I believe it would be best if Mme Korsakova took it upon herself to make the arrangement. – I cannot think of anyone else who could do this well, apart from me."

Peter Ilyich Tchaikovsky 1873.

This quotation referred to his *Symphony No. 2. Opus 17, (The Little Russian)*.

In 1873, Tchaikovsky visited the Rimsky-Korsakov's in St. Petersburg and played the finale of this work. It was so greatly received that he wrote, *"the whole company almost tore me to pieces with rapture."*

Nadezdha had, in 1871, successfully arranged his overture *Romeo and Juliet* for four hands and *"begged with tears in her eyes"* to do the same for this finale as she had for the overture. However, it was not to be. Ill health prevented her from doing so and Tchaikovsky made the arrangement himself.

Nadezdha was acknowledged as a brilliant pianist and especially talented in adapting orchestral scores for the piano (four hands). She had been tutored in this by the composer Alexander Dargomyzhsky and had transcribed not only works by Tchaikovsky but also scores by Borodin, Glazunov and her husband, Nikolai. She also arranged vocal scores including Borodin's *Prince Igor* and Nicolai's *The Maid of Pskov* and *The Noblewoman Vera Sheloga.*

Although having been born nearly 30 years after Clara Schumann, in Russia rather than Germany, Nadezdha's life was determined in much the same fashion as had been the lives of Clara, Fanny Mendelssohn and Maria Mozart. She had shown early talent; been given a good musical education; had performed in soirées in private houses, and composed three operas before she was married.

Yet the inevitable happened. Her husband's career took precedence even though she was far better trained, musically, than he. Her life was dedicated to furthering his career, rather than her own, and naturally, as a wife she was expected to run the home and bear his children. However, due to her excellent tuition she became a musical partner to him as well as a domestic one and as great an influence as Clara Schumann had been to Robert.

Nadezhda Nikolayevna Purgold was born in St. Petersburg in October 1848. Her father Nicolai was a wealthy connoisseur and of his ten children, two showed musical talent, Alexandra as a singer and Nadezhda, a pianist.

Nadezhda started playing the piano at the age of nine and in the mid 1860's studied at the Saint Petersburg Conservatory, but did not graduate. Her tutors were Anton Gerke for piano, Nikolai Zaremba for music theory, and later, Rimsky-Korsakov for composition.

The Conservatory was, at that time, a fairly new establishment founded in 1861 by Anton Rubinstein, the Russian pianist and composer. Rimsky-Korsakov joined the faculty in 1867 and since 1944 it has been called the N.A. Rimsky-Korsakov Saint Petersburg State Conservatory. During his decades at the Conservatory he taught many composers who eventually found musical fame. These included Prokofiev, Glazunov, Stravinsky and Respighi.

During the 1860's and 70's Nadezhda played piano at musical

soirées in her own home and the home of Dargomyzhsky. It was at these soirées that she met Mussorgsky and Borodin and began to play their music as well as that of Mili Balakirev, another member of *The Five.*

Mussorgsky became a special friend to both sisters and called Nadezhda, *"our darling orchestra."*

The group of composers called *The Five* met in St. Petersburg during the period 1856 –1870. They were also known as *The Mighty Handful.* Balakirev led the group that consisted of César Cui, Modest Mussorgsky, Nikolai Rimsky-Korsakov and Alexander Borodin.

The main objective of these five composers was to create music that was traditionally Russian rather than European. This nationalistic movement, based on heritage and folklore, was to be found in many spheres of the arts at that time.

It was at Dargomyzhsky's house in 1868 that Nadezhda met Nikolai. They found that they had much in common and it wasn't long before *The Five's* musical circle began to organise soirées at the Purgold home.

Nikolai became a frequent visitor and was also invited to stay with the family at their summer residence in Lyesnov. He was not considered to be a ladies man but in Nadezhda he found a beautiful and capable woman, strong minded, with artistic views and great talent. In him she found warmth and tenderness.

Once, on leaving her, during their courtship he wrote, *"I thought about you a great deal on the way – and when I happened to see something nice, I always wanted you to look at it with me."*

In December 1871 he proposed, and they were married in July 1872. Nikolai was 28, Nadezhda nearly 24. Mussorgsky acted as best man. Their honeymoon took them to Switzerland, the Italian lakes, Milan and Venice. When they returned they settled in an apartment in Shpalernaya Street in St. Petersburg.

Nikolai Andreyevich Rimsky-Korsakov was born in March 1844. His place of birth was Tikhvin, east of St.Petersburg and his ancestry was aristocratic. His father Andrey was the third son of Lieutenant-General Peter Voinovich Rimsky-Korsakov.

Nikolai's mother was his second wife, the illegitimate daughter of a wealthy landowner, but well educated and very musical. It was through her that his interest and love of folk music began.

His mother was, however, 18 years younger than her husband. A year after their marriage, in 1822, she gave birth to a son, Voin, She then had no more children until Nikolai was born in 1844, creating a gap of 22 years between the brothers. Even so they were very close, Voin becoming almost a father figure to his younger brother.

Nikolai showed an interest in music from an early age and had regular piano lessons from the age of six. His parents considered his love of music, *"a prank"*, but even during his schooldays at the School of Mathematical and Navigational Sciences in St. Petersburg, he continued his lessons, went to operas and played four-hand music with his friends. He also developed a passion for the orchestra.

His family had a Naval background and his brother, eventually, became a rear admiral. Voin's letters home excited the imagination of his younger brother and he devoured books about the sea. It was inevitable that he should also join the Imperial Navy.

When he was not at sea he continued his musical studies and in 1861 his piano teacher introduced him to Balakirev and thus the other members of the Five. It was listening to their opinions and considering their encouragement that he began to create a musical career alongside his naval duties, and so doing met Nadezhda in 1868.

He found her to be a quiet woman with great talent and very artistic views. He said little about his feelings to his friends but it was obvious that she was beginning to play a very important role in his life and becoming a great influence in his musical development.

Nadezhda, as previously mentioned, had already written three operas, one of which, *The Enchanted Spot,* she finished only a week before her marriage. This had been based on Nikolai Gogol's, *Evenings on a Farm near Dikanka.* Gogol was a Russian novelist and dramatist, born in the Ukraine and considered to be the father of Russian realism.

Nadezhda was very enthusiastic about Gogol's work and on the evening of their betrothal, she and Nikolai read his *May Night* and Nadezdha hoped to persuade him that this would be an interesting subject for an opera.

Although Nikolai had a few ideas for this, initially, it wasn't until 1877 that he settled seriously to the task and completed the opera in 1879, one of 15 eventually written.

After their marriage Nikolai's friends, especially Balakirev, found Nadezhda to be a demanding critic of her husband's work and began to wonder if her influence was leading him astray from the musical preferences of The Five.

As previously mentioned, it was in 1871 that Nikolai became Professor of Practical Composition and Instrumentation at the St.Petersburg Conservatory. Mikhail Azanchevesky, who had recently taken over as Director, wanted new skills and enthusiasms in all musical subjects. It was this professorship and its financial security that encouraged Nikolai to marry and settle down.

He was, however, very aware of his technical shortcomings and during his first few years was as much a student as his pupils, but with Tchaikovsky's assistance in harmony and counterpoint he soon became an excellent teacher.

Nadezhda gradually gave up composing after her marriage, building up, instead, a prominent social life as accompanist and performer at soirées. She also travelled with her husband, attended rehearsals and helped in the arrangements of his compositions and those of other composers.

Their first child Michael (Misha) was born in August 1873 and Tchaikovsky dedicated his Cradle Song to Nadezhda in anticipation of his birth.

He was the first of seven children and was followed by Sofia in 1875, Andrey in 1878, Vladimir 1882, Nadezhda 1884, Margarita 1888, and Slavchik 1889.

Andrey studied philosophy at university, became the founder editor of the first Russian music magazine and eventually taught Music theory and History at Leningrad University. He married the composer Yuliya Veysberg, wrote a five volume study of his father's life and work and established a museum in his name. One chapter in the book he devoted to his mother.

His sister Nadezdha married the composer and teacher Maximilian Steinberg, in 1908, rated by Nadezhda (her mother) as a greater composer than Stravinsky.

As with many large families at that time, death amongst children was unfortunately quite common. The Rimsky-Korsakovs always spent the summer outside St. Petersburg, where they hoped the fresh country air would benefit the children and also Nadezhda, whose many pregnancies had taken their toll on her health.

1890 was an especially hard year for the family. Nadezhda became seriously ill with diphtheria and Andrey also became infected. Then in December the baby Slavchik died and soon after two-year old Margarita (Masha) fell ill. Time spent in Switzerland and the warmth of the Crimea did not aid the little girl's recovery and she died in August 1893 having been ill for two and a half years.

His family troubles and ill health greatly affected Nickolai causing creative droughts and depression. In the same year, 1890, he began to suffer from *angina* and in 1892 another medical diagnosis confirmed *neurasthemia,* a nervous illness causing rushes of blood to the head, memory loss, confusion and oddly unpleasant obsessions.

He considered giving up composition permanently but Tchaikovsky's death in 1893 opened up the opportunity to write for the Imperial Theatres, and with his creativity restored, he wrote 11 operas between 1893 and 1908.

Eventually, however the angina and stress of these later years gradually wore him down. In 1905 a Revolution took place in Russia causing political unrest and dissatisfaction with the government. This resulted in military mutinies, strikes, terrorism and peasant revolts.

Nikolai was removed from his position at the Conservatory because he supported 100 students who were expelled for taking part. The police banned performances of his work, but when other professors and over 300 more students walked out in support of him, he was reinstated.

His controversial opera *the Golden Cockerel* was a direct result of this. It criticised the monarchy and Russian Imperialism and its first performance, an adapted version, was delayed until 1909, a year after his death.

Nikolai died in Lyubensk and was interred in the Tikhvin Cemetery at the Alexander Nevsky Monastery in St. Petersburg.

Stravinsky, who attended his funeral, wrote, *"I will remember Rimsky in his coffin as long as memory is. He looked so very beautiful I could not help crying. His widow, seeing me, came up to me and said: "Why so unhappy? We still have Glazunov." It was the cruellest remark I have ever heard and I have never hated again as I did at that moment."*

Nadezhda, whose tact had often been in question was not afraid to speak her mind, although, at her husband's funeral it seemed rather out of place from a mourning widow.

After her husband's death she became executrix to his estate, editing and publishing his posthumous literary and musical works. It was a laborious and painstaking task and included the collection of articles, notes on music and correspondence with his friends that eventually became *My Musical Life.*

She took on a solo role of guarding her late husband's artistic interests, dealing, alone, with his business arrangements in the publishing and theatrical worlds. She was ever conscious of preserving his legacy and protested strongly when Diaghilev sought to use music from *Scheherazade* and *The Golden Cockerel* in his ballets.

She also collected, in two archives, relics connected with her husband's life. One is to be found in the State Public Library in Leningrad, the other, in the form of a gift from the Rimsky-Korsakov family to the museum of the Leningrad State Conservatory was later transferred to the Philharmonic Museum, in 1930.

She published two recollections of Dargomyzhsky in 1913, and wrote a memoir of Mussorgsky. Cui, Tchaikovsky, Borodin, Mussorgsky, Glazunov and Lyadov all dedicated works to her.

Nadezhda outlived her husband by 11 years and died at the age of 70, from smallpox.

Surviving autograph manuscripts are: -

The Bewitched Place – a symphonic tableau after Nicolay Gogol and dedicated to Musorgsky.

Midsummer Night – an opera, in piano-vocal score, piano pieces and songs.

A Scherzo in B flat, for piano.

14. Alma Mahler (1909)

15. Gustav Mahler

Chapter 5

Alma Mahler

1879 - 1964

"You must subordinate every detail of your future life to my needs, and want only my love in return. – From now on you have only one job: to make me happy."

Gustav Mahler - 1902

Before she was 20 Alma had written more than 100 songs, some instrumental pieces and the synopsis of an opera. Music was the one element in her life that she took seriously and for which she showed promise and ability, yet two years later she married Gustav Mahler, 20 years her senior, and agreed, at his demand, to take on the role of wife and promoter of his work, sacrificing her own creativity for a man whose music she did not even like. *"The fact is that he thinks nothing of my art and much of his, while I think nothing of his and much of mine."*

This marriage came as a surprise to those who knew Alma, for she was intelligent, had great beauty and was courted by many. It was obvious that she was impressed by Gustav's standing in the musical world. He was an ambitious man, had been director of the Court Opera (the *Hofoper)* in Vienna since 1897, and had already built up a reputation as a composer.

Thus Alma's musical career, not unlike that of Nadezhda

Rimsky-Korsakov, came to an abrupt end, primarily due to the male expectancy of a woman's role as wife and mother. Only when, some years later, their marriage was in difficulties, did Gustav relent, regretting his former attitude in the hope of saving their relationship by encouraging Alma to prepare some songs for publication. His own publisher, Universal edition, issued five of these in 1910.

However, a year later Gustav died, ending their short marriage of nine years and leaving Alma a widow at the age of 31.

Alma Maria Schindler was born in Vienna on August 31st, 1879. Her father, Emil Jakob Schindler was a reputable landscape painter, her mother, Anna von Bergen, a former singer who gave up her career to devote herself to her husband.

Emil was a dreamer for whom painting was an obsession. He wrote of his work, *"My collection of painted canvases represents the small result of great inner struggles and passions, jokes begotten of tears, and elegies born from smiles."*

He was fortunate enough to receive the backing of wealthy patrons and as orders poured in so the material life of his family improved and they were able to live in luxury and comfort in a romantic castle on the outskirts of Vienna.

Alma adored her father who read Goethe to her at the age of eight, but despised her mother. She had a younger sister Grete whom she later discovered was not Emil's daughter, but the result of her mother's brief affair with a man possibly suffering from syphilis.

Grete made several attempts to commit suicide and ended up in an asylum. She came to a tragic end when the Nazis put her to death, along with many others considered to be mentally sick.

As sisters Alma and Grete grew up happily in their privileged environment until the sudden death of Emil at the age of 50 from an intestinal obstruction. Alma was heartbroken. She was then only 13.

After her father's death her mother married again. Her new husband, Carl Moll, had been a former pupil of Emil's. Alma found this hard to take and refused to allow him any authority over her, as a parent. He was, however, a talented painter who played a leading role in Viennese artistic life being one of the co-founders of the Vienna Secession, a group of artists who desired to create a new style outside the confines of tradition. He was also a Nazi sympathiser and at the end of the Second World War committed suicide.

Alma rarely attended school but was educated privately under her mother's supervision. She read widely, learnt Greek, and studied the philosophies of Nietzsche and Plato. Her music teachers were Joseph Labor and Alexander Zemlinsky. She studied counterpoint, was a student of scores and knew much of Wagner's repertoire by heart, singing it in a pretty mezzo-soprano voice.

One of her father's friends, Max Burckhard, a director of the Burgtheater, Vienna, encouraged her reading, bringing her plays by Ibsen and other classical writers. He also chaperoned her to the Mozart Festival at Salzburg as well as to the opera and theatre in Vienna.

Both Burckhard and Zemlinsky were suitors for her hand, for Alma's attractions, her fair hair and piercing blue eyes along with her demanding intelligence and wide interests, were very evident. If she had a flaw it was a slight deafness in one ear caused by a childhood illness.

However when she met Gustav she was swept away by the presence of this man of 41 who was a major figure in the life of Vienna.

He was shorter than her, wore thick spectacles, had a mop of dark hair and a deep, powerful voice. He was noted for his tempers and absent-mindedness, yet ruled his orchestra with an iron hand.

Gustav Mahler was born a German Jew in Kalischt, Bohemia on 7ᵗʰ July 1860, the second of 14 children. His father was the proprietor of a distillery. His childhood memories were of hardship and poverty, of a mother desperately struggling to cope with her meagre resources and the loss of her children, eight of whom died young.

His parents spotted that Gustav had talent when he was six and arranged piano lessons for him. When he was 15 he was admitted to the Vienna Conservatoire and three years later moved to Vienna University where he studied history and philosophy as well as music.

His career as a conductor began in 1880 at a summer theatre at Bad Hall. From this he took posts at a variety of opera houses including Vienna, Prague and Budapest. Amongst the operas he conducted were Wagner's *Der Ring des Nibelungen*, Weber's *Die drei Pintos* and Mozart's *Don Giovanni*. He then spent six years at the Hamburg opera from 1891 –1897 until his eventual move to the most prestigious musical position in Austria as director of the Vienna Opera.

In preparation for this role Gustav had converted to Roman Catholicism. Under Austro-Hungarian law no Jew could occupy the post. This was no great hardship. Over the years he had found much to interest him in Catholicism, which was portrayed in his music along with works stimulated by his Jewish upbringing.

He met Alma at the house of Berta Zuckerkandl, who was a well-known hostess and journalist. He remarked to Burckhard, *"She is an interesting and intelligent girl. At first I didn't like her and took her for a doll. One doesn't as a rule take seriously girls as young and pretty as she is."*

As for Alma she summed up her impressions of him in her diary, *"I must say I liked him enormously. Of course, he is terribly nervous. He paced around the room like a wild animal. He's pure oxygen. You get burnt if you go too near."*

Their formal betrothal took place in December 1901, and they were married on March 9th 1902. It was a very private affair, attended by close family, to avoid publicity, and was held in the vestry of Karlskirche. The couple then journeyed to Russia and spent their honeymoon in St. Petersburg. They were the recipients of great hospitality even dined with the Duke of Mecklenburg, a member of the Imperial family. Gustav also gave three successful concerts for which he received a handsome remuneration.

Their home was an apartment in Auenbruggergasse where

Gustav had formerly lived with his sister Justi. Even though he earned a good salary Alma discovered that they were very short of money. Gustav had spent it all on building a house at Maiernigg where he composed when on holiday.

This house was a sturdy wooden chalet built on a slope with a beautiful view overlooking a lake. In a small bungalow nearby he installed a piano and worked on his compositions. During the first summer that she spent there Alma found her life monotonous and lonely. Apart from the walks with Gustav and trips on the lake she was very much on her own. She wrote, *"My mind is torn with conflicting impulses. Left to suffer on my own, I long to find someone who would think of me, help me to find myself. --- I sit down at the piano, dying to play, but musical notation no longer means anything to me. My eyes have forgotten how to read it. I have been firmly taken by the arm and led away from myself."*

Back in Vienna Alma, who had always lived in luxury, took over the finances, discovered that she was a born organiser and drew up a plan to pay off her husband's debts.

Their lives became routine. Gustav spent his mornings at the opera, came home for lunch, took long walks with Alma in the afternoon then returned for an operatic performance in the evening, followed by dinner.

Here in Vienna she was not completely alone. She had her family around her and enjoyed visits from a few friends, that is, the ones that Gustav could tolerate.

In 1902 her first child was born. It was a difficult birth. They named her Maria Anna, (nickname - Putzi). A second daughter Anna Justine (Gucki) was born in 1904. Anna became a sculptor and lived to be 84. Sadly Maria died at the age of four from diphtheria.

The marriage was turbulent. Alma had constant privations imposed on her by Gustav. *"My discontent increases hour by hour. I must start reading again, learn something. I must have an inner intellectual life, as I used to. --- How full my life was once, how empty now."*

Theirs was a difficult relationship, Gustav seemingly unaware of how to deal with Alma's moods and she desperately searching for some animation in her dull existence. From being a wealthy, sparkling and admired young woman in society she found herself hemmed in, secluded from any social life and with little money to spend.

In May 1907, after ten years at the Vienna opera, Gustav resigned. He was, by that time, hated by many of the musicians because of his critical treatment of them. They were upset because he did not introduce new works, except his own, and accused him of being a victim of his own inflated ego. His music was greatly criticised and he was often under attack in the anti-Semitic columns of the press.

It was only a month later, at Maiernigg, that Putzi, aged four and a half fell ill. Diphtheria was a fatal disease, there was no vaccine for it, and after 14 dreadful days and a final tracheotomy to help her breathe, she died.

It was a terrible tragedy. Alma spent many days in bed distressed with shock, and Gustav was heartbroken at the loss of the little daughter who had most resembled him, with a head of black curls and a very determined nature. Even little Gucki was haunted all her life by the fact that her sister's death was somehow her fault.

It was a time for change. The house at Maiernigg was sold. It would always hold unbearable memories.

Gustav decided to accept a generous offer from the Metropolitan Opera in New York to spend three months a year for four years conducting the New York Philharmonic Orchestra.

"I am taking my homeland with me," he said to the Zuckerkandl's, as they waved goodbye, and sailed from Cherbourg, happy to leave Vienna, its sorrows and stresses behind, and optimistic about their prospects in a different part of the world.

Gustav immediately settled enthusiastically to his work, leaving Alma alone in a country whose language she could not speak. Her daughter, Gucki had been left behind with her grandmother and Alma found the days endlessly long. She wrote home constantly and succumbed to phantasy illnesses.

However one illness did prove to be more than a psychological illusion. She suffered a miscarriage, and her depression grew.

Gustav, to help her recover, accepted invitations from several Americans, one of whom was Otto Kahn, a financier and patron of the Metropolitan, another Doctor Fraenkel, president of the Neurological Society. In this way Alma, who blossomed in society, gradually brightened and began to bask in her husband's obvious success.

For Gustav being well received was welcome after his treatment in Vienna. He wrote to his mother in law, " – *everyone is so full of good wishes and gratitude for the few things I have so far been able to do. I live like a prima donna. I feel that I am someone important and hope that America will continue to treat me well.*"

In April, at the end of their first season, they travelled back to Vienna, deciding that the experience had been a success and welcoming the time when they would return.

They moved into a house in Toblach, South Tyrol. The summer of 1908 was described by Alma as *"the saddest and most painful we had ever or would ever spend together --- full of sorrow for the child we had lost, full of worries about Mahler's health."* He had been diagnosed with a heart disease, (infective endocarditis) shortly after Putzi's death.

Their second season in New York was again rewarding. This time four year old Gucki and a governess went with them. They had a suite in the Savoy on Fifth Avenue. Gustav's health improved even though he had to share his conducting role with Toscanini. The two men couldn't stand each other. As for Alma she thoroughly enjoyed being swept into the fashionable whirl of New York society. However, she once more suffered a miscarriage.

Their marriage was on the rocks. Alma seemed always to be surrounded by admirers and on their return to Europe, having left the excitement of her fashionable life in New York behind, she complained of *nervous troubles* and went to a spa at Levico with Gucki and Miss Turner, the governess. Gustav wrote her moralising letters that did not improve their relationship.

Soon, however they were thrust into another season in New York. Their social life was boundless. Invitations poured in. They even dined with millionaires and their popularity did not wane even though Gustav's eccentricity manifested itself in early departures from gatherings, surprising outbursts or a stubbornness to open his mouth.

On their return they stayed with the Molls whilst Gustav and Carl searched for a house. Once again Alma complained of *nervous troubles* and her doctors, finding no cause for this, advised another spa, this time at Tobelbad, a place that was very much in fashion.

It was here that she met Walter Gropius. He was 27, handsome, fair-haired and from a respectable Prussian family. It was the summer of 1910 and he was at the start of his career as an architect. An affair began that would fluctuate over the next ten years.

Alma did not leave Gustav for Walter, even after he had discovered her infidelity. Maybe this was because she knew how desperate he would become if she did.

As for Gustav he was persuaded that he was going to lose Alma and sought the wisdom of Freud. After hours of talking, Freud told him that in his opinion Gustav had been seeking a wife who resembled his mother, a woman who had been weary and care-worn, compliant with her husband's and family demands. Likewise Alma, in marrying a man 20 years her senior, had been looking for the father figure that she had dearly loved.

This diagnosis brought about a great transformation in Gustav's attitude towards her that she found overwhelming. In a letter to Gropius she wrote, "*I am experiencing something that I would not have believed possible. His love is so boundless that my staying here – in spite of all that has happened – means life, and my going away death to him --.*"

It was during this period, as previously mentioned, that Gustav encouraged Alma to publish some of her songs.

During the winter of 1910 they spent their fourth season in New York. Even though the affair with Walter sizzled in the background, the relationship between Alma and her husband seemed to improve. He bought her a solitaire for Christmas costing 1000 dollars and organised a ceremony for her on Christmas Eve where gifts were piled on a table strewn with roses. Alma seemed to be holding the upper hand, and enjoying the subservience of her obsequious husband. She wrote, *"At that time we were very united."* When her mother came to stay she found her daughter very cheerful and in the best of health. She had given up alcohol, and even started to compose again.

But this did not last. Gustav's days were numbered. In February 1911 he began to suffer from sore throats and raging temperatures. Doctor Fraenkel diagnosed a form of endocarditis, which was an inflammation of the lining of the heart due to a streptococcal infection.

They decided to return to Europe where a new serum had been developed. Gustav was placed in a clinic and a bacteriologist from the Pasteur Institute, Professor André Chantemesse agreed to minister it to him. However the treatment had little effect. They returned to Vienna, at Gustav's request, where he died peacefully in hospital, at the age of 51, on 18th May 1911.

He was buried next to his daughter Putzi, in the cemetery at Grinzing, outside Vienna. It was Gustav's wish to be buried in silence and a simple monument erected bearing only his name. It did, however, develop into a large affair attended by friends and colleagues and a curious, respectful crowd who stood in the rain to study the heaps of flowers that surrounded his grave. His friend Bruno Walter, the conductor, described his funeral thus, *"-- we laid the coffin in the cemetery at Grinzing, a storm broke and such torrents of rain fell that it was almost impossible to proceed. An immense crowd, dead silent, followed the hearse. At the moment when the coffin was lowered, the sun broke through the clouds."*

Alma did not attend the funeral on her doctors' advice. They considered her to be completely exhausted after the months of tending Gustav in his struggle for life.

For six months convention demanded that she remain out of society. She did not wear mourning according to Gustav's wishes, and was well provided for money. The Opera paid her a pension, Gustav had left her 100,000 dollars in New York and 139,00 crowns in Vienna. There was also a plot of land on the Semmering, that they had previously designated for a house.

Her role in life now became that of Gustav's widow. There was deference in her treatment, an aura that settled around her as a seal of respect for the widow of a great man.

During his lifetime, as well as being a leading orchestral and operatic conductor, Gustav had composed symphonies and songs. He died before his tenth symphony was completed. *Lieder eines fahrenden Gesellen* (Songs of a Travelling Journeyman) and *Das Lied von der Erde* (The Song of the Earth) are his principal song cycles.

His compositions were never really accepted by the musical culture of Vienna at that time, and were greatly criticised. He has since been acknowledged as an important late Romantic, early Modernist composer.

In the autumn of 1911 Alma left the Moll's house and moved, with her daughter, Gucki, to a house in Elisabethenstrasse, a house that was completely hers to furnish and design to her own tastes.

After the six months mourning period she began to make appearances at concerts and to accept the respect given to her as Gustav's widow.

Her admirers' seemed to queue up at the door. Doctor Fraenkel proposed marriage and a biologist, Paul Kammerer threatened to commit suicide on Mahler's grave if she did not respond to his love.

However in January 1912 Alma joined Walter Gropius in Berlin and was introduced to his mother and sister. The women, from very different backgrounds, did not like each other and Alma returned home unsure of her relationship with Walter and refusing to answer his letters.

It was at this time that Carl Moll introduced her to a painter, Oskar Kokoschka. He was 24, and a little strange, with oblique eyes, ears that stuck out and the belief that he had inherited second sight from his mother and grandmother. His pictures exhibited a brutal, violent style and, because of this he was not achieving much success.

He had been commissioned by Carl Moll to paint Alma's portrait. An affair started between them during which Oskar continuously pressed her to marry him, but Alma constantly refused having no desire to give up her position as the widow of a famous man.

"I'll marry you," she said, *" when you have produced a masterpiece."* In fact Oskar did just that. He produced a painting called *Die Windsbraut* (The Tempest – or Bride of the Wind). It hangs in a museum in Basle and depicts a couple lying in an enormous seashell in the middle of a raging sea. The couple, of course, were Alma and Oskar.

Alma organised the building of her house on the Semmering in which they lived together. The relationship did not last. After having one abortion she became pregnant again, deciding, this time, to keep the baby, that is, until the arrival, one day, of Gustav's death mask. Oskar could not tolerate its presence especially as Alma exhibited it in a prominent position. After an extremely violent row Alma, once again, went to a clinic for an abortion. Oskar was distraught but still clung on hoping for an improvement in their relationship.

Then, in 1914, the First World War broke out, and Alma pressurised Oskar to join up. Eventually he was accepted in the cavalry and having, hopefully, disposed of this lover, Alma then rekindled her affair with Walter Gropius.

Walter was also in the military and Alma, with time on her hands started to compose again and offered some of her Lieder to Gustav's publishers. They were not interested.

She received many letters both from Oskar and Walter. In one letter Oskar wrote, *"I love you and am holding on to you, whatever you think, whoever you are and wherever you are."*

But it was Walter's marriage proposal that Alma accepted. Having been given two days leave they were married on 18th August 1915, without informing his mother. However, when Alma became pregnant, for the seventh time in her life, a transformation took place in the attitude of her new mother-in-law. Alma was soon to be the mother of her son's child and Frau Gropius was full of concern for her welfare. Alma, enjoying the situation, did her utmost to be absolutely charming towards her.

As for Oskar, Alma wrote in her diary, " *he has become a strange shadow for me – I have no further interest in how he lives. And yet I loved him.* "

Oskar survived the war, even though he was wounded twice. He moved to Britain, as the Nazi's considered his art to be degenerate. He wrote many times, over the years, to Alma, the last time being on the occasion of her 70th birthday. He became famous not only for his Art but also as a poet and playwright and died in Montreux in 1980.

On the fifth of October 1916 Alma gave birth to a little girl who she called Manon, after her mother-in-law.

Walter was not given leave to be there and Alma began to lose patience with their distanced partnership. *"I've had enough of this makeshift existence,"* she wrote. *"My love for Walter Gropius has given way to a tired twilight-marriage. No marriage can be carried on at a distance."*

She began to build up her social life once more, holding Sunday *salons* in Vienna or on the Semmering, attracting artists such as Gustav Klimt; musicians, Arnold Schönberg and Anton Berg, and writers, Franz Blei and Franz Werfel.

A relationship developed between Alma and Franz Werful although she was the elder by ten years. Franz had been born in Prague, where his father owned a glove factory. He was a carefree, talkative man who chain-smoked, drank too much and loved the pleasures of life.

When he met Alma he was already a published poet. He had spent part of the war in the artillery and the army press service in Vienna. He was a Jew, a pacifist and a social democrat. Physically he was rather plump, shorter than Alma, with vivid blue eyes and a charming personality.

Alma became pregnant again at the age of 39. This time she had no intention of having an abortion even though she knew that the father of her child was Franz. Walter, not knowing of her affair believed the child to be his.

A baby boy, Martin, was born prematurely. When Walter eventually discovered Alma's infidelity and that he was not the father he agreed to a divorce if he could have custody of Manon. Alma refused. The divorce was eventually granted on 12th July 1919 on the terms that Walter could see Manon regularly.

Although she was free to marry Franz, Alma was reluctant to do so. She was 40 years old, had her home and children. When she married Walter she had lost her widow's pension and any income derived from Gustav's works was minimal. Post war times were tough. Food was rationed but Alma, always able to cope with practical matters managed to provide a stable home for her family.

Gucki who preferred her proper name Anna, was now 15, an adolescant. She had grown up having been obliged to live with the variety of men in her mother's life. She had bright blue eyes in a solemn face, was a proficient pianist and showed great pride in her father's achievements. She was patient and caring towards her little half-sister, Manon, who was already a charming replica of her mother.

As for the baby Martin, he was extremely delicate and developed hydrocephalus, an accumulation of fluids on the brain. He had an operation, a cranial puncture, but died when only 10 months old.

Alma's relationship with Franz continued. His post war support of an Austrian Republic caused him to be wanted by the Police, but Walter, four times wounded and twice awarded the Iron Cross, came forward to act as his guarantor.

Franz was then able to develop his career. His plays were performed in Vienna, Leipzig, Prague and Munich, but they earned him little money.

Alma still would not marry him. The difference in their ages worried her, especially when her daughter Anna became engaged, at the age of 17, to Rupert Koller, the son of family friends. She was not thrilled at the thought that she might soon become a grandmother.

The political scene remained unsettled and Alma bought a house in Venice, *Casa Mahler*, as a possible refuge. Although they spent periods of time apart Alma accompanied Franz on lecture tours to Egypt and Palestine and they were also together in Berlin for the premiere of Berg's opera, *Wozzek* that he had dedicated to Alma. The opera was well received.

It was later to be performed in Prague, a city that was no longer Austrian but the capital of Czechoslovakia. Franz and Alma once again attended this with the Bergs. Here things were different. The premiere took place on the same day as the funeral of the Bürgermeister of Prague who had, unfortunately succumbed to a fatal stroke whilst watching the dress rehearsal. This stimulated protests to break out and Berg, not Franz was the recipient of, *"Shame on you! Jew! Jew!"* They left under police protection, stunned at this reaction especially as Berg was not Jewish and his wife happened to be the illegitimate daughter of Emperor Franz Joseph.

Life in Vienna, indeed Austria, was difficult. Repressive government measures provoked a general strike, but along with the political unrest, Alma had to face worries at home. In 1929 her daughter Anna went through divorce proceedings for the second time. After Rupert Koller she had married a young composer, Ernst Krenek.

In that same year Alma reached 50. Although she carried a little more weight, she enjoyed the modern fashions of showing her elegant legs in silk stockings, and her looks, framed now by shorter hair, still turned many eyes.

It was during this year that she eventually decided to marry Franz. The wedding took place on the 8th July 1929. Their honeymoon was spent in Egypt, Palestine and the Lebanon. Alma found the squalor and misery in this part of the world, abhorrent, but it inspired Franz, who wrote a historical novel, The *Forty Days of Musa Dagh,* based on the Armenian genocide that took place in 1915 by the Turks. This novel, first published in 1933, became his first great success and earned him consideration for a Nobel Prize.

Alma now found herself a leading hostess in Vienna, married to a well-known, prosperous writer and living in a 28-room house on the Hohe Warte.

Her daughter Manon, at the age of 13, showed promise of a beauty akin to that of her mother, but Anna's life was still in turmoil. She had been married and divorced for the third time to Franz's publisher Paul von Zsolnay, had a daughter, Marina, and finally, with some success, embarked on a career as a sculptor. In 1937 she won first prize at the World Exhibition in Paris.

But the rise of Hitler and the Nazi party was to be the downfall of Franz. He was convinced that he would be accepted into the Nazi Association of German writers and signed a declaration of loyalty to the regime. All he wanted was for his works to be read and accepted in Germany, but the Association turned him down and the German authorities ordered his work to be burnt. Gustav's works were also banned.

It was during these difficult times when refugees from Germany began to arrive in Austria and the social democracy of the country was on the verge of destruction that another family tragedy occurred.

Manon, at the age of 17, was struck down with poliomyelitis. Walter came from London to spend a week with her. She was confined to a wheel chair and the doctors were hopeful that she would recover the use of her legs, but, after a few months she died, suddenly, on Easter Monday, 1935. The funeral took place at Grinzing, hurriedly, for fear of the spread of contagion and was commemorated by Alban Berg who wrote a violin concerto *Dem Andenkin eines Engels*, in dedication to her. Translated, it means, *To the memory of an angel*.

Alma was genuinely distressed at the loss of her third child. She knew she would have no more, and felt burdened by age. Her hair was now white and she dressed mostly in black.

In 1936 she sold her house in Venice. It seemed full of Manon's presence. Her life was spent in travel with Franz, who, basking in his current success was in demand outside Austria, for interviews, talks and monologues.

It was when they were travelling in Italy in 1938 that the news came of the imminent annexation of Austria by Germany, the *Anschluss*. Franz was fortunate to be out of the country, at the time.

Alma hurried back to Vienna, without him, giving no warning of her return except to her maid, Ida. She wanted to persuade her daughter and mother to leave.

She went to the bank and withdrew all her liquid assets and sewed them in a belt for Ida who was to take the money to Switzerland. She packed a few bags, not forgetting Gustav's manuscripts and arranged for any works of art to be taken to Carl Moll's house. He was to be her trustee. She failed to persuade her mother to leave her husband. As previously mentioned Carl was a supporter of the Nazis, and welcomed their arrival into the city.

At least Alma managed to get her daughter, Anna, to agree to leave, pointing out that, as Gustav was her father, her life could be in danger. The journey back was torturous. They had to push their way onto trains and travelled via Prague, Budapest, Zagreb and Trieste until they finally reached Milan, where poor Franz was waiting for them, half-dead with worry.

From Milan they went to Zurich, to Franz's sister where they met up with the faithful Ida who handed over the money that she had smuggled out in her belt. They eventually settled in France, from the summer of 1938 until the Spring of 1940. Their home was a converted watchtower at Sanary-sur-mer.

When war was declared they knew that they would have to leave. They were foreigners in a small town, with Czech passports, speaking French with an Austrian accent. They travelled to Marseille hoping to get a boat to the United States, but they hadn't got a Visa, and knew that the Germans, having marched into Paris, would soon be invading the rest of France and that anyone found to be Jewish would be transported to concentration camps.

Their salvation came in the form of an American journalist, Varian Fry, a representative of an organisation called the Emergency Rescue Committee, instigated by the United States Government on behalf of Eleanor Roosevelt, wife of the president. Her purpose in creating this organisation was to obtain emergency visas for artists, writers and scientists who were stranded in territory taken over by the Nazis.

The Werfels were included in this group and so grateful for any assistance. However acquiring a visa to enter the United States was not enough. They still needed the French Government to grant them an exit visa, and this they would not do. French border officials were obliged to hand over refugees to the Germans.

There was only one alternative, a clandestine escape over the border into Spain via the Pyrenees. A young American guided the group that also included a German family, the Mann's.

It was a long, exhausting and traumatic trek on foot but they finally reached their goal, met up with Varian Fry and their luggage, continued on to Portugal and eventually found passage on a Greek boat heading for the United States.

They settled in Los Angeles, were fortunate that Alma was able to draw on some money that Gustav had deposited in a bank in New York. Also Franz started writing again and produced a book, *The Song of Bernadette*. He had been spiritually moved by a visit to the shrine of the Virgin Mary at Lourdes, where they received great kindness from the Catholic community during their time as refugees. This book's success was later made into a film starring Jennifer Jones, and Franz became a well-known author in the United States.

He was never as settled as Alma in their new country. He could not cast off Vienna and his homeland as readily as she. He succumbed to a series of heart attacks, missing the première of the film of *The Song of Bernadette*.

On 25th August 1945 Alma found him dead at his desk. He was 56 and had lived just long enough to know that Hitler was dead and that Germany had surrendered to the Allies.

Now Alma, at 66, was alone and growing increasingly deaf. In 1946 she became a US citizen and decided to travel to Europe. She stopped off in London to visit her daughter and granddaughter. Anna had married for the fourth time, a conductor, Anatole Fistoulari.

Alma's main objective, however was to see Vienna again. She found the destruction of the city horrifying, the Opera, Burgtheater and cathedral all in ruins. Her house on Hohe Warte had also been partly destroyed by American bombs and her home on the Semmering sold to the Soviet authorities.

Anna, Alma's mother had died in November 1938 and Carl Moll had not kept his word. Everything that Alma had left in his charge had been sold and, as before mentioned, on the day that the Red Army entered Vienna he had committed suicide, with his daughter and son-in-law.

Alma settled in an apartment in New York, looked after by the faithful Ida. She did not take up her music again but rebuilt her role as Mahler's widow. His place in musical history was now assured, whereas Franz Werfel's popularity was already diminishing.

Her tenacity was evident, her appearance majestic, dressed always in black and adorned with elaborate hats and countless jewels she occupied a definite position in the musical world and was guest of honour at all the concerts in which Gustav's music was part of the programme. In 1959 Benjamin Britten dedicated his *Nocturne for Tenor and Small Orchestra* to her.

On 11th December 1964, at the age of 85 she died of pneumonia, holding her daughter's hand. She had been confused in her mind for the last year of her life and also refused treatment for diabetes. She was buried in the cemetery at Grinzing alongside her daughter Manon.

Alma had been, in effect, a legend in her lifetime. She published two very frank autobiographies about her life, one in 1940, the other *And the Bridge is Love* in 1959, but many of her accounts about her life with Gustav have been discovered to be false and misleading.

Tom Lehrer wrote a song called *Alma*. Also novels and plays have been written about her, and films made, the most notable being the 2001 Bruce Beresford film *Bride of the Wind* and the novel of the same year, by Max Phillips called, *The Artist's Wife*.

As for her compositions only 17 songs survive. 14 were

published during her lifetime, five in 1910 at the time when Gustav attempted to rekindle their marriage and allow her to compose again. Two other collections appeared in 1915 and 1924. It is believed that after this date she ceased to compose. Three other songs were discovered posthumously, two of which were published in the year 2000.

Hugo Wolf and Zemlinsky influenced the style of her compositions that contained bold, chromatic harmonies similar to early songs written by Schoenberg. Some are still performed and recorded today.

Her music manuscripts and personal papers are to be found at the University of Pennsylvania and at the Austrian National Library in Vienna.

When Gustav, in 1910, whilst trying to rebuild the collapse of their marriage, encouraged Alma to publish her songs, she did this with little enthusiasm. *"Ten years of wasted development cannot be made up anymore,"* she wrote. *"It was a galvanised corpse that he wanted to resurrect."*

The composer that Alma had wished to be in her early years, had been suppressed, her desire to create, lost in years of discouragement, and her talents left unfulfilled.

Instead she is known mostly as a woman who surrounded herself with *geniuses.* She wrote in her memoirs, *"God granted me the privilege of knowing the brilliant works of our time before they left the hands of their creators – and if I was allowed to assist these knights for a while, then my existence is justified and blessed."*

Published Works by Alma Mahler

Five Songs for Voice and Piano – 1910
1. *Die Stille Stadt* (The Quiet Town – Dehmel)
2. *In meines Vaters Garten* (In My Father's Garden – Hartleben)
3. *Laue Sommernacht* (Mild Summer's Night – Falke).
4. *Bei dir ist es traut* (With You It Is Pleasant – Rilke).
5. *Ich wandle unter Blumen* (I Stroll Among Flowers – Heine).

Four Songs for Voice and Piano – 1915
1. *Licht in der Nacht* (Light In The Night – Bierbaum).
2. *Waldseligkeit* (Woodland Bliss – Dehmel).
3. *Ansturm* (Storm – Dehmel).
4. *Erntelied* (Harvest Song – Falke).

Five Songs for Voice and Piano – 1924.
1. *Hymne* (Hymn – Novalis).
2. *Ekstase* (Ecstasy – Otto Julius Bierbaum).
3. *Der Erkennende* (The Recogniser – Franz Werfel).
4. *Lobgesang* (Song Of Praise – Dehmel).
5. *Hymne an die Nacht* (Hymn To The Night – Novalis).

Posthumously Published for Voice and Piano – 2000
1. *Leise weht ein erstes Blühn* (Softly Drifts a First Blossom – Rilke)
2. *Kennst du meine Nächte?* (Do You Know My Nights? – unknown author).

16. Ottorino and Elsa Respighi in the garden
of their Rome villa I Pini, 1933

Chapter 6

Elsa Respighi

1894 - 1996

"My soul-searching was long and merciless; and only when I was absolutely convinced that I could renounce the life I had led until then, and my work itself, and dedicate myself entirely to his life and his work – only then did I, without any reservations, accept his proposal."

Elsa Respighi from her book
50 Years of a Life in Music 1905 – 1955

It was whilst studying at the National Academy of St.Cecilia in Rome that Elsa became a student in the class of fugue and composition taught by Ottorino Respighi.

Her early years had been filled with the singing of her parents, and her education highlighted by piano lessons. Music was her world. She lived for *"nothing but music"*. Her growth into adult life was focused solely on her love and need to explore its creation.

It was not an easy decision, to agree to marry her tutor, a man 14 years her senior, with the prospect of having to give up her own musical ambitions. However, she was not forced to forego her abilities, as had Alma Mahler, but to adapt them with those of her husband. Hers was not a step away from music but a diversion whereby she became supporter, critic and promoter of her husband's work.

Although she gave up composition Elsa developed her singing and travelled extensively with Ottorino, from 1920 until 1932. Theirs was a partnership. They performed together in about 350 chamber concerts in Europe and America, the programmes including songs composed by Elsa as well as Ottorino, and containing larger orchestral works written by him.

Their 17-year marriage ended in 1936 when Ottorino died. Elsa lived to a great age devoting herself to the promotion of her husband's music. She initially completed his unfinished opera *Lucrezia* and, riding on its success, continued with composition. However much of this she did not complete devoting herself to writing prose rather than music that included a biography of her husband's musical life, on which she worked for 18 years.

Elsa Olivieri-Sangiacomo was born in Rome, on March 24th, 1894. Her parents were Arturo Oliviera Sangiacomo, an army officer, and Maria Canobbio Tamés. She was the oldest of five children, the youngest being born eight months after her father's death in 1903.

From 1900 until 1902 the family lived in Florence. At the age of six Elsa began to study the piano, encouraged by Arturo. He was a great lover of music. Elsa's early recollections, as an infant, were of her father intoning Wagner themes, in his beautiful voice, and her mother singing Mexican lullabies in her native tongue. Maria had been born in Mazatlán on the Pacific coast of the Mexican state of Sinaloa.

Maria did not have any special talent for music but, to please her husband, she started to learn the guitar and eventually was able to accompany Arturo's singing, and the duets that Elsa sang with him.

Maria's modest musical contribution was of great benefit to the family when, at times, they did not have the use of a piano.

Arturo's dream was to resign from the army and this he achieved in September 1903. He then devoted himself to writing and journalism, becoming one of the editors of *La Tribuna*.

The family moved to Rome and settled in a beautiful, well furnished house on the Via Cavour. It was a house where *"happiness lived."* Every morning the children would waken to the sound of their father's beautiful voice singing as he dressed.

In 1903, Elsa began studying piano with an excellent musician, Clotilde Poce. She soon discovered that she disliked the formality of learning scales and set pieces, preferring to create her own. In a letter to her father, her mother wrote:

"Elsa is in front of me, and do you know what she is doing? She has taken a sheet of music paper and she is writing down a few notes --- according to her, she is composing a sonata. From time to time she gets up and goes to the piano to hear the motif of the notes that she has written."

Sadly, this happy situation did not last. On Christmas Day, of that same year, Arturo died. Maria was then only 28, had four children and was expecting another, to be born the following September. Elsa, the oldest, was only nine.

Because of this tragedy the children were dispersed amongst relatives. Elsa lived, for two years, with her maternal grandparents who cared for her physical needs but gave her little affection.

In 1905 Maria was able to reassemble her family in Rome. She rented an apartment, helped by her parents, who gave her an allowance of 100 liras per month. Unfortunately her father cut off this allowance on hearing that her brother's wife Mimmi and her five-year-old daughter had also moved in. Mimmi had been left destitute by a husband who had squandered away all their money and possessions.

Elsa resented their intrusion and the demands that this placed on her mother, neither did she forgive her grandfather for his severity. Gradually, however, she grew to love Mimmi who became her beloved "auntie". It was Mimmi who compiled a diary that acted as a family chronicle for the years between 1905 and 1955.

Mimmi described Elsa's suffering following her father's sudden death.

"Elsa, because of her exceptional precocity, has suffered tragically from her father's death. The infinite sadness that can

be read in her beautiful face is really striking. --- Her body has not taken the immense pain and grief well, and for a few months now a nervous stomach has been tormenting her and has forced her to keep a very severe diet."

For many years a deep sorrow reigned in the family. Mimmi could see the deep attachment that Elsa felt towards her mother and brothers and noticed her sad, thoughtful expression, and lack of enthusiasm in studying the piano.

However this sombre time eventually passed. Elsa wrote, " *– when the deep sorrow for father's death had lessened, I began to bloom again in the house now made gay by the unfettered happiness of my younger brothers."*

Her musical studies continued. In 1905 she was enrolled in the National School of Music.

She found the whole atmosphere of the school and building depressing. It wasn't until the school moved to the Palazzo del Grillo and Pietro Mascagni became its director that her attitude changed and she began to take a greater interest in studying.

Mascagni, young, handsome and already famous was idolised by his students, including Elsa, especially as his colourful life was full of scandal and lawsuits against editors.

During these years Elsa found great pleasure in singing, especially with others. *"In the chorus my whole being seemed to be struck by the sounds, and my soul seemed to expand, to dilate in the multiplicity of voices."*

One of her greatest joys was to go to the church of St. Alexis and listen to the monks singing Gregorian chants.

Her mother supported Elsa in her love of music and attended concerts with her at the Academy of St. Cecilia, and recitals at St. Peter's Cathedral.

Many artists appeared and works of famous composers were performed.

Symphonies by Beethoven and Brahms greatly impressed her, as did *Till Eulenspiegel* by Richard Strauss and Bach, played on the cello by Pablo Casals. Also imprinted on her mind was the violin music of Fritz Kreisler.

She also witnessed the achievements of rising conductors such as Toscanini and Mahler.

She studied the piano with Giovanni Sgambati, an eminent musician and outstanding teacher. He recognised Elsa's talents and began preparing her for concert performances.

It was two days before her performance in a concert at the Russian Embassy that Elsa felt a cramp in her right arm. This was diagnosed as "pianist's cramp" and was caused by an acute inflammation affecting the nerves of the arms. This was devastating for Elsa as it continued for many years and, at the age of 16, shattered her hopes of becoming a concert pianist.

But there were other musical possibilities open to her. She had always been interested in composition. Against the advice of family and friends who thought it unrealistic for a woman to aspire to compose, she applied and was lucky enough to be accepted for one of the vacant spaces in the class of advanced harmony. Here, as the only female, she worked hard for three years and graduated in advanced harmony and counterpoint with the intention of gaining admission, as previously mentioned, into the class of fugue and composition taught by Ottorino Respighi.

There was great excitement amongst the students at his appointment in January 1913. Elsa then in her third year of advanced harmony, knew and loved some of his songs. She wrote, *"Someone who had seen Respighi – had passed on to us that he was very young, bore a strange resemblance to Beethoven, had a bright smile, and was very pleasant."*

In 1914 the First World War began. Times were hard but Elsa's mother, Maria, managed wonderfully to acquire the bare necessities on which to keep the family fed. One of Elsa's brothers, Georgio, who was only 15, caused his mother considerable worry because he was desperate to enlist in the Army.

Elsa took a course and became a Red Cross nurse working at the Leoniano Hospital. Mimmi wrote, *"She is truly attractive in her white uniform, ---with a few reddish blonde curls peeking out from her cap, and with those clear eyes (greenish or grey) which contrast with the dark skin of her face."*

Certainly, at this time her life was full of activity and Mimmi described her as *"strong willed, poised, talented, full of life, unselfish and creative."*

It was this creativity that inspired her to have a little stage built in the chapel on the ground floor to give shows to the injured soldiers. In this she persuaded many of her friends to help.

Mimmi describes Christmas thus :-

"It was completely filled with soldiers. Beautiful music was coming from high in the choir loft where a small organ was located. Respighi played the organ. --- Elsa was singing. I could not hold back my tears, as I looked at so many suffering sons who were openly and intensely moved. Everything had been organised by the tireless Elsa, and once more I was reminded of how much that creature could give of herself to others."

It wasn't until October 1915 that Elsa finally enrolled in Respighi's course for Fugue and Composition. She found the three years of study absorbing, due to his unique qualities as a teacher. He did not impose his personality on to his students but helped them to find their own means of expression. When Elsa showed him a song that she had written, based on a Spanish text his comment gave her great inspiration, *"This, you see, young lady, is your path. You must continue to compose in this direction."* He even insisted on taking some of her songs, when he went to Milan, to show them to the publisher Ricordi.

On June 2nd, 1917, Elsa took her final exam that included conducting a set of songs, *Tre canzoni*, for voice and orchestra. She considered conducting a kind of martyrdom. *" They could have played the violin upside down and I would not have known it."* Her instructions to the orchestra were, *"My friends, play the best you can because I cannot do anything to help you."*

Musical life in Rome struggled during the war years. Many members of orchestras and choirs enlisted, and performers and composers cancelled their visits and concerts.

A highlight for Elsa, however, was when Ottorino told her that the songs that he had taken to Milan had been accepted for publication.

This joy was overshadowed by the fact that her brother, Georgio, who, as previously mentioned, had volunteered for the Army at the age of 16, was seriously ill and had been sent to the Leoniano hospital for treatment.

By 1918 Elsa was finding the many activities in her life extremely taxing particularly the organisation of shows for the soldiers. Eventually she gave up her service in the hospital, and her English lessons, devoting herself to her music studies that had, because of her nursing, been pushed back into the evening hours.

Her final work to be performed at St. Cecilia's was a symphonic poem *Serenata di maschere*. It was about a carnival night when the clowns go serenading.

Ottorino was obviously impressed by Elsa's hard work and she overheard him discussing her with some of his friends. *"All the other students who are taking their final examination in composition complain constantly about this or that. She is the only one always happy and cheerful, She never asks for anything. She probably deserves a kiss."*

To his surprise Elsa appeared and responded, " *Well, Maestro, if my work is successful, you will give me a kiss as a reward."*

So it was that her symphonic poem was very well received and the kiss sought and accepted, with great pleasure.

A few days later Ottorino proposed. It was a shock. Elsa's admiration for him had always been as a student to a tutor. She spent the summer in a little mountain town called Tivoli agonising over her decision, assailed by doubts about their difference in age and character, whilst receiving daily letters from him full of tenderness and love. This inevitably affected her, brought them closer together and after much soul searching, she accepted his proposal.

Ottorino Respighi was born in Bologna, Italy on 9th July 1879. His father was a piano teacher and taught his son to play both piano and violin. He grew to be a rather reserved boy with obvious talent.

He studied violin and viola at the Liceo Musicale in Bologna with Federico Sarti, also composition with Giuseppe Martucci and musical history with Luigi Torchi, who was a scholar of early music.

By the age of 20 he had become a brilliant viola player and in 1900 composed his first major work, *The Symphonic Variations*, for his final examinations.

Such was his talent that after receiving his diploma, he applied and was offered the position of principal violist in the orchestra of the Russian Imperial Theatre in St. Petersburg, during its season of Italian opera. He later also played at the Bolshoi theatre in Moscow.

Whilst there he became fluent in Russian, showing an aptitude for languages, and spent five months studying composition with Rimsky-Korsakov. Many of Respighi's brilliantly orchestrated scores owe much of their colour to the mentoring of this Russian master.

He also studied composition with Max Bruch in Berlin, in 1902. Returning to Bologna he gained a second degree in composition and then, until 1908 played as first violinist in the Mugellini Quintet.

He then spent some time performing in Germany until finally turning his attention to composition. He settled in Rome, in 1913, after his appointment as teacher of composition at the Conservatory of St. Cecilia, where Elsa was one of his students.

The war was coming to an end. Their engagement was short and they were married on January 11th, 1919. Elsa was 24, Ottorino 39.

After a brief honeymoon, in a villa loaned by a friend, they moved into a two-roomed apartment in Otterino's former lodgings.

Adapting their different working habits was difficult. Ottorino taught in the morning then came home to work in the afternoon. Elsa had never been an early riser, found motivation difficult in the morning and so by the time she was ready, her husband had returned and she was unable to disturb him.

Instead she started singing lessons again.

In the summer of 1919 they rented a villa, in Capri. It was

completely isolated, in a magnificent setting and they were able to enjoy the beautiful scenery and talk of their hopes for the future. Elsa admits that she was *"still very much in awe of my Maestro!"*

It was in Capri that Ottorino wrote many songs that he asked Elsa to sing. She was desperate to please him, yet he very rarely handed out praise. At times, driven to tears, he would comfort her, tell her to have faith in her abilities and soon they would be giving concerts together. *"That was my dream,"* wrote Elsa.

Her dream was fulfilled. As previously mentioned, between 1920 and 1932 they gave over 350 concerts together in many countries in Europe, and North and South America.

In May 1921, Mimmi wrote in her diary, after reading reports on their long tour of Austria, Hungary and Czechoslovakia, *"All the clippings mention my niece's perfect training, the fine timbre of her voice, and her extraordinary musicality. Others expound with many words of praise for the composer.*

--- the audiences must have perceived not only the study Elsa and Ottorino continually pursue together, but the beautiful and profound accord that binds them."

They led an exhausting life, travelling, rehearsing, composing and performing. On returning from North America in 1927, Mimmi wrote, *"I found Elsa dead tired. As I listened to what they had done during their trip in America, I wondered how this child – tormented for months with colitis and, at the beginning of each spring, with hay fever, bears up under so much fatigue. But I am aware of her extraordinary ability to bounce back, and I think that a few weeks will be enough for her to be in full form again, ready to leave."*

Such was their life, lived in the fulfilment of their music. Elsa's youth and indomitable will was often needed to lift her husband from bouts of discouragement. It was her supreme faith in his abilities that would eventually overcome his despair and would render him calmly happy to return to work. Only then did she relax and succumb to her own exhaustion.

During their travels they met a variety of musicians. In Vienna it was Alma Mahler described by Elsa as " *a personage, a symbol of Vienna --- a very beautiful lady of exceptional quality."* They also met the pianists Arthur Rubinstein and Paderewsky, and the guitar player Segovia.

Their fame and popularity grew. Their concerts were sell-outs. Many premieres of their work took place in the United States and on one notable occasion Elsa walked out on to the stage for the premier of a song cycle, *Deita Silvane,* to find that an eminent group of musicians, Toscanini, Horowitz, Rubinstein and Heifetz were sitting together in the front row. With great calm she delivered her performance and afterwards was congratulated by Toscanini, *"But you know, you sing very well."* There was no doubt that this was praise indeed from the great man whose charisma enthused orchestras to perform the most thrilling music.

They decided to move outside Rome to a villa called I Pini, set in the peace of the countryside with a view that reached to Mount Soratte. It was their ideal home and the garden was Elsa's pride and joy.

In the house were exhibited many of the gifts that they had received on tour. On a table lay a gold medallion made by the sculptor Viligiardi and amongst the silver objects presented to them from many different countries was a large silver platter from Argentina that rested on the piano.

Elsa wrote, " *Our lives at I Pini were the happiest yet. In that house, in that park which totally fulfilled our desires and dreams of many years, we had reached perfect harmony, an unnameable happiness that kept us far from the realities of life."*

In the April of 1935 whilst in Budapest for the premiere of his opera, *La Fiamma,* Ottorino developed a high fever, severe sore throat and could hardly swallow. The diagnosis was edema of the epiglottis. An operation to avoid suffocation was avoided, the fever subsided, a slow recovery followed. The after effects of possible deafness filled him with horror. A trip to Vienna was turned down but one to Prague was undertaken causing Otterino to realise his lack of stamina from which he suffered headaches and fatigue.

At the end of 1935 he was beset by another fever. Blood

tests showed blood poisoning and the onset of endocarditis, an inflammation of the membrane that lines the heart, a streptococcal illness for which there was no cure.

Elsa nursed him at I Pini, watching his slow decline. Mimmi helped her as well as her mother, who had travelled from her home in Mexico. Elsa rarely slept and became incredibly weary. Mimmi wrote of her, "*I saw how much effort it took for her to lift her arm and with infinite mercy offer a glass of something to Ottorino or to guide her rigid robot-like steps in one or another direction. But she remained unchanged until the last moment, incredibly feigning serenity with a smile on her face.*"

Ottorino's final moments came, on the 18th April 1936, during a violent storm. Mimmi wrote, "*Right after his last breath, the sky turned clear and a nightingale began to chirp from a cypress right in front of his room.*"

Almost immediately the exhausted Elsa was given a powerful sleeping pill that rendered her unconscious for 24 hours.

The funeral that she had organised was modest. There were no escorts, flowers or music, just a hearse bearing a single wreath of laurel from the park, and the name – Elsa.

The following year Ottorino's remains were reinterred with honour, in the city of Bologna, the place of his birth.

Ottorino Respighi was a composer greatly famed during his lifetime. His death at the age of 56 left several pieces of work unfinished. He is most famous for his brilliant orchestrations particularly in his *Roman Trilogy: Fontane di Roma* (Fountains of Rome), *Pini di Roma* (Pines of Rome) *and Feste Romane* (Roman Festivals). He also orchestrated works by other composers including Bach, who he admired immensely, Monteverdi, Vivaldi and Rossini.

With Elsa, he developed a great interest in Medieval and Renaissance Italian music from the 16th to the 18th centuries. One composition resulting from this was *Antiche arie e danze perliuto* (Ancient Airs and Dances) for the lute. He also introduced Gregorian plainchant into works such as his *Concerto Gregoriano, Vetrate di Chiesa (Church Windows)*.

Elsa collaborated with him on the ballet version of *Gliuccelli* (1927) and an arrangement of the Bach *Passacaglia* (1930 – 31).

From 1923 – 1926 he became director of St. Cecilia's Conservatoire in Rome and was elected to the Royal Academy of Italy in 1932.

Elsa, widowed at the age of 42, continued her life in the promotion of her husband's music. She returned to composition and, as previously mentioned, finished his opera *Lucrezia* with the assistance of Ennio Porrina, one of Ottorino's former students, who had based his style on that of Respighi. Its premiere was at La Scala on 24th February 1937.

Elsa's creativity thus stimulated she continued to compose during the difficult years of the war. *Il pianto della Madonna,* a sacred drama, in 1938, was written from a text by Angelo Poliziano, an Italian Renaissance poet. She also composed a symphonic poem, *Serenata di maschere* and several orchestral suites.

However, her prize winning one act opera *Dona di Alcesti* (1942) was never performed: a three act opera, *Samurai* (1945) remained unpublished and another opera, *Sciusciai, figlio del cielo*, was never finished.

She continued to travel, attending concerts in promotion of Ottorino's work, many of which were held in his memory.

When the Second World War seemed imminent she moved out of *I Pini* to a four-room apartment on Via Panama. She was far more comfortable in this smaller environment than in the large sixteen-room villa that held so many memories.

The villa was then let to the Ministry of Foreign Affairs, but when the Germans entered Rome it was standing empty. With Elsa's permission they occupied the villa, but not as she would have wished, and destroyed much of its beauty. Trucks were driven over her garden of box trees and roses. The structure of the building was damaged by alterations, and Ottorino's study partitioned into four rooms. When the Allies finally won the war they also occupied *I Pini* in a similarly destructive way. All of this practically broke Elsa's heart.

After the war she travelled to Mexico via the USA, to visit her mother and brothers who had settled there. Whilst in Washington she presented the manuscript of *Le Fontane di Roma* and the mask of Ottorino to the Library of Congress.

Wherever she travelled she was greeted with great respect. With Ottorino she had made a great impact on the musical world in the Americas.

Whilst in Los Angeles she was hosted by Walt Disney who showed her personally around his studios, and spent many pleasant hours with Edward G. Robinson.

She also met Alma Mahler again describing her as extraordinary, a widow for the third time, reverting to the name of the first, and most renowned of her husbands, Gustav Mahler.

Elsa had crossed the Atlantic 16 times, by sea, and now, being able to fly home was most welcome when she eventually returned to Italy.

It was inevitable that her mother and aunt expected her to remarry and she did receive many marriage proposals. In her diary Mimmi wrote, *"There is also her mother's desire to see her settled. To which, every time the discussion is brought about, Elsa answers, "Mother, marriage is something else, something important. I do not deny that I may like so-and-so enough to flirt with, but to marry them, no."*

Two years later, in 1954, Aunt Mimmi died. Elsa was very sad at losing the person to whom she had been very close since the age of 11 and who had understood and supported her for so many years.

She began to become disillusioned, uninspired by the musical scene in Rome and turned her creativity to prose. She wrote or collaborated in five works, the first of which, in 1954, was a biography of her husband, *Ottorino Respighi: dati biografici ordinati* that was translated into English in 1962.

She also wrote an epistolary novel, *Venti lettere a Mary Webs*, in 1957 that was told entirely in letters written by each character to one another.

In 1975 she produced *Cinquant'anni di vita nella musica*, Fifty

Years of a Life in Music 1905 – 1955. This book was a memoir of her musical life with Ottorino that describes their work, tours and the many influential people and musicians that they met.

Her final work, in 1978, was *Il teatro di Respighi* in which she collaborated with Leonardo Bragaglia.

In 1969 she established Fondo Respighi in Venice, an organisation founded to promote musical education in Italy.

She was at the forefront in the organisation of celebrations for Ottorino's centenary in 1979, in which some of his neglected works were performed and recorded for the first time.

Since then some of her own works, for solo voice and accompaniment have been published.

Elsa lived for 60 years after the death of her husband, dying on 17th March 1996, a week before her 102nd birthday.

In the musical life of 20th century Italy it is Ottorino Respighi whose name is honoured as a famous composer, his works that are performed and published. After her marriage, Elsa gave up her own hopes for a career as a composer, and willingly adapted her musical skills to the needs of her husband forming a partnership that was hugely successful in both America and Europe.

In the words of her aunt Mimmi, *"The union of Ottorino and Elsa was a masterpiece. To that happy association Ottorino brought his great talent as an artist, and Elsa all the rest. Without Elsa to cheer him on, Respighi would have left fewer beautiful operas to the world. Without Respighi, Elsa would probably have had a less splendid life, but she would still have amounted to something."*

Compositions

Il Pianto della Madonna, a sacred drama,1938. Text by Angelo Poliziano.

Alcesti, a one act opera, 1941. Text by Guastalla.

Tre canti corali for a capella choir, 1944. Text by Guastella.

Caterina da Siena, a cantata for soprano and chamber ensemble. 1945. Text by Guastella.

Samurai, a three act opera. Text by Guastella.

Fior di Neve, a fairy opera in 3 Acts.

Serenata di Maschere, a symphonic poem,

Intermezzo Romantico for viola, flute and harp.

She also wrote several orchestral suites.

17. Jessie Coleridge-Taylor and the children.

18. Samuel Coleridge-Taylor with his family.

Chapter 7

Avril Coleridge-Taylor

1903 - 1998

"Quite early in life I began to feel a sense of music within me that was anxious to make its way out. Not only did I want to write music – as I had seen my father do – but to express myself through beautiful sound. So, before I was 12, when most other children amused themselves by playing games, I was concentrating on composition."

The Heritage of Samuel Coleridge-Taylor
by Avril Coleridge-Taylor

Avril was the daughter of composer Samuel Coleridge-Taylor who died suddenly in 1912, when she was only nine. She had been devoted to her father, would lie in bed at night listening to him play the piano knowing that she wanted to follow in his footsteps and also become a professional musician and composer.

But, due to her origins, (she was a quarter black African), she experienced prejudice in her life, as did her father. Avril recalls how he reacted, when they were out walking one day, and a group of local youths shouted abuse at the colour of his skin. *"When he saw them approaching along the street he held my hand more tightly, gripping it until it almost hurt."*

However, Samuel was proud of his origins and wrote many compositions that contained Afro-Caribbean elements.

After her father's death Avril was forced to live under the dominance of her mother, who favoured her brother, Hiawatha. Fortunately, in 1915, her talent won her a scholarship to study composition and piano at Trinity College. She was able to build up a successful musical career, wrote over 90 works, some of them under the pseudonym of Peter Riley, and became renowned as a conductor, founding several orchestras and ensembles.

It was when she travelled to South Africa in the 1950's, as a conductor, that she experienced, first hand, the prejudice caused under apartheid. This affected anyone of black ancestry, even though, as in her case, she was only one-fourth black.

On her first visit she was a guest conductor, but when she returned, seeking employment, things were very different. *"No broadcasting or other arrangements would be available to me on account of South African policy towards people of colour, or of mixed parentage."*

She had no choice but to return home.

Gwendolyn Avril Coleridge-Taylor was born in South Norwood, London, on 8th March 1903. Her father was the composer Samuel Coleridge- Taylor, her mother, Jesse Fleetwood Walmisley, a pianist who had met Samuel whilst training at the Royal College of Music.

Samuel's father, Daniel Peter Hughes Taylor, 1848 -1904, was a Krio, born in Sierra Leone, in West Africa. His mother was an Englishwoman, Alice Hare Holmans 1856 -1953.

In the early 1870's Daniel had come to England to study medicine at King's College Hospital Medical School. After qualifying he became an assistant in a medical practice in England but became disillusioned in the way he was treated, due to the colour of his skin, and returned to Sierra Leone. In the 1890's he became coroner for the British Empire in Gambia, but his health deteriorated rapidly and he died at the age of 56. It is probable that he was unaware of his son's existence.

Samuel was born on 15th August 1875 at 15 Theobalds Road,

Holborn London, described by Dickens as *"the dingiest collection of shabby buildings ever squeezed together."* He was named after the poet Samuel Taylor- Coleridge.

Whether his mother and father were married is disputable, but later Alice moved to Croydon and married a railwayman, George Evans.

Her family, the Holman's were highly musical and encouraged Samuel's interest, giving him his first violin and lessons. Alice and George had three more children who were also musically trained, one, Victor became a professional musician.

Even though Samuel suffered at school due to his colour, (nicknamed *"Coaly"*), he was fortunate enough to be encouraged by several benefactors. The first was Joseph Beckwith, a local violin teacher and also conductor of the orchestra of an amateur theatrical society. Joseph had met Samuel in the street playing marbles whilst in possession of a small violin. When encouraged to play the violin (not marbles), Joseph recognised that he had talent and became his first teacher.

His second benefactor was Colonel Herbert A. Walters who was an army volunteer, silk merchant and amateur musician. In this capacity he was honorary conductor of St. George's Church, Croydon. He had a good relationship with the local schools and when the headmaster of the British School in Croydon mentioned the small coloured boy who was particularly fond of music, he encouraged him to join the choir. It was obvious to Colonel Walters that this boy was exceptionally gifted. Samuel sang treble with the choir for many years, after which he moved, when his voice broke, with the Colonel, to the church of St. Mary Magdalene, in Addiscombe.

It is likely that the Colonel's interest in Samuel was due to the fact that he had been an acquaintance of his father, and he was proud to see him blossom under his patronage, especially when he sang a solo, *"There is a green hill far away,"* in Exeter Hall on 18th June 1888, and received a standing ovation.

Along with his singing Samuel was building up a reputation as a talented violinist. The Colonel was determined to encourage his ability so that he didn't end up in a dead end job, (he was known for influencing his city friends to help members of his choir seek suitable employment).

In 1890, he arranged an interview with Sir George Grove, Principal of the Royal College of Music. This interview resulted in Samuel, at the age of 15, being awarded a scholarship as a student of the violin. He would also study piano, organ, theory and composition.

His tutor for composition was Charles Villiers Stanford who was a reputable composer and showed a unique skill in his teaching, was sensitive to his pupils and their problems and won their loyalty with his warm personality. He was yet another benefactor aware of Samuel's talent and was also conscious of his racial problems. In general, within the sanctum of the college, Samuel was accepted for his worth rather than his origins, but, on one notable occasion, out of envy, a jealous student handed out a racial insult akin to ones he had previously heard on the streets of Croydon. Stanford, passing by, put his arm around Samuel's shoulders and led him away. In his room he offered words of consolation and support saying that Samuel had *"more music in his little finger than (the offending student) had in the whole of his body."*

Avril wrote, *"No wonder he had such a deep admiration for his professor's teaching and guidance."*

Even though Samuel was a talented player, his main intention was to become a composer. In 1892, whilst still at college, he wrote some anthems that Novello accepted for publication. One of these, *Break forth in joy*, he dedicated to his benefactor Colonel Walters.

At the College of Music he found himself amongst a number of promising students including, Gustav Holst, Thomas Dunhill and Ralph Vaughan Williams. In 1893 he was awarded a composition scholarship and in 1895 and 1896 won the Lesley Alexander Prize for composition.

On 5th July 1894, at a student concert his *Nonet in F minor* was performed. In the audience Sir George Grove nodded with satisfaction, and said, " *Good! Very promising,*" but also added,

"He will never write a good slow movement until he has been in love."

As if on cue, a few months later Samuel met and fell in love with Jessie Walmisley, a pianist for whom he wrote a special composition.

In 1896 he met the poet, Paul Lawrence Dunbar, the son of a slave. Paul's tough upbringing, experiences and success as a poet inspired Samuel to delve into a study of Afro-America culture, and their collaboration resulted in several pieces of music including the song cycle *Seven African Romances*, in 1897 and an operatic romance, *Dream Lovers* in 1898.

Unfortunately Paul Dunbar's life was short and he died in 1906.

In the year of 1898 Samuel reached a pinnacle in his career brought about this time by Sir Edward Elgar who found himself unable to accept a commission to produce work for the Three Choirs Festival. This festival brought the choirs together of the three cathedral cities of Gloucester, Hereford and Worcester and was a platform for many aspiring composers. Elgar recommended that Samuel take his place. *"He still wants recognition and is far away the cleverest fellow going amongst the young men"* (Avril in The Heritage of SCT).

Grateful of the opportunity Samuel wrote *Ballade in A minor*, a melodic piece echoing Tchaikovsky and Dvorak. It was an immediate success.

In the same year *Hiawatha's Wedding Feast* was premiered, based on the poem by Henry Longfellow. The poem was already very popular and Samuel's score had been published well ahead of its first performance. The music was described as light and airy, exotic with feathers, skins and colourful names, and the melodic tunes bursting from a bank of massed voices filled listeners with emotion and excitement. Samuel conducted the premiere and received a great ovation.

During the following 15 years *Hiawatha's Wedding Feast* was performed hundreds of times in the United Kingdom alone.

The sequels' demanded by his admirers, *The death of*

Minnehaha, 1899 and *Hiawatha's Departure,* 1900 never echoed this initial fame.

On December 30th 1899 Samuel married Jesse. They both lived in Croydon and had become practice partners, playing duets on the violin and piano.

Jesse's parents were not overjoyed that their daughter wanted to marry a coloured composer but despite opposition the wedding took place at Holy Trinity Church, South Norwood. The couple then honeymooned in Shanklin on the Isle of Wight, lived, for a short while in lodgings, before moving to 30 Dagnall Park, South Norwood where they stayed until 1901. They then made their final move to 10 Upper Grove. Their son, Hiawatha was born in 1900 and Avril, named Gwendolyn, in 1903.

Samuel's reputation grew, making his workload, over the years until his death, almost impossible. It included conducting, composing and teaching. From 1904 he was conductor of the Handel Society and at the time of his death was a lecturer at Croydon Conservatoire, the Crystal Palace School of Art and Music, the Guildhall School of Music and was Professor of Composition at Trinity College.

In 1904, 1906 and 1910 he toured in North America. His popularity and that of *Hiawatha's Wedding Feast* was enormous, especially amongst the black population who were triumphant at the progress of a coloured musician. Back home, many who formerly slighted him for his colour became suddenly proud to know him.

It was not only his popularity that enforced a heavy work load, but his need for money to support his family. He received only a small one-off payment when a work was published and it was only after his death that the system of royalties was adopted that gave the composer a percentage of the profit every time the work was performed.

On September 1st, 1912 Samuel died from pneumonia complicated by exhaustion through overwork. He was 37 years old. Avril, who adored her father, was heartbroken. She had been sent to stay with her granny during the three days of his illness and after he died her granny told her, *"he will never wake again."* Avril then cried out, *"but he must – he must."*

Intense pain filled her heart as she remembered their walks in the countryside, his humming of tunes that he was writing and their trips, on the train, to the Guildhall, where he taught. *"I remembered the way in which people greeted him with friendly smiles as we walked along together,"* she wrote. *"I felt so proud of being with him, for there were so many who loved him."*

His funeral became a great public event. Samuel had disliked the black of mourning and Avril was dressed in white with a black velvet ribbon around the brim of her hat. Hundreds of people lined the route and waited outside the church, climbing on railings for a better view. Inside the packed church *"When I am dead, my dearest"* was performed by Julien Henry, who had often sung for Samuel, and the slow movement from his Violin Concerto was played. A huge crowd followed the cortege on its three and a half mile progress to Bandon Hill where Samuel was buried in a small cemetery near Beddington in Surrey. Many times the procession was halted as traffic stopped and bystanders stood beside their vehicles removing their hats and bowing their heads. Avril wrote, *"Each and every person irrespective of their status paid their personal tribute to the beloved composer on his last journey."*

Samuel had not died a wealthy man. His annual income in the year of his death was estimated at less than £200. Jesse gave the impression that she was penniless, and King George V granted her a pension of £100 in recognition of her husband's work. A memorial concert was held that provided a tidy sum for the family, especially, as previously mentioned, no royalties were received from the performance of any of Samuel's compositions.

Hiawatha's Wedding Feast continued to be popular during the 20's and 30's, championed by Sir Malcolm Sargent who conducted 10 seasons of a ballet version at the Royal Albert Hall. These were immensely popular, involved hundreds of singers and created a spectacular scene. In 1933 Avril joined the *corps de ballet* (incognito) and was amazed at Sir Malcolm's skill as a conductor. *"He felt and breathed every movement so that the music and dancing were as one."*

These productions came to an end due to dissension between the copyright holder and the producer. Many people had made money out of this magnificent work except for the composer and his family. Initially Samuel had sold it to Novello's for 15 guineas.

Although this piece was his most famous accomplishment he also wrote a variety of vocal and instrumental music, and included Afro-Caribbean elements that demonstrated his pride in his African descent. His achievements initiated a change in the attitude towards black musicians, especially in America.

His reputation increased in the immediate aftermath of his death and Jesse gloried in this fame. She was a force to be reckoned with, had shown definite fighting instincts when insults, due to Samuel's colour, had been hurled at him. Avril always longed for her mother to show more restraint and dignity, but this did not suit her dominant personality.

Avril's father had always shown her love, care and kindness, whereas her mother seemed to openly want to control her and Avril was too timid and naive to do any other than obey her. *"After Father died, I found that I was being domineered by Mother's forceful nature. But I never questioned her right to exercise this power. Indeed I was much too timid to think otherwise, so that I acquiesced in whatever was demanded. As a consequence my girlhood was governed by the whims of this one possessive parent."*

It seems that when she was five her mother had tried to have her adopted, taking her to meet a lady and gentleman in a large house. When the gentleman had lifted her up and asked her, *"How do you like your new father?"* Avril's response had been to cry loudly for her real father so much so that the plan for adoption did not go ahead.

On another occasion Jesse attempted to send her to boarding school. Avril wrote, *"Immediately father replied: "If you do that then the boy must go too." That settled the question once and for all. Nothing would have induced her to part from her son."*

After her father's death Avril's life was one of exhausting routine. She had many chores forced upon her including cleaning, cooking, and running errands. She attended a little private school, when allowed, but found that she slipped way behind the other students, due to absence, and she had to work twice as hard to catch up. Also to save expensive travel costs her mother made her journey the three and a half miles by bicycle.

She often stopped off at the cemetery, where her father was buried, to place some wild flowers on his grave. Her late arrival at school went unadmonished by the principal who recognised the sorrow on her tear-stained cheeks, and realised how much she mourned a father who she had dearly loved.

Avril always had a good relationship with her brother and, not long after her father's death they both attended classes at the Guildhall School of Music. Landon Ronald, who had greatly admired Samuel's work and wished to encourage his children, had arranged this. Hiawatha showed promise as a violinist but lacked the ability to concentrate. Unfortunately neither of them made much progress.

Fortunately for Avril another friend of Samuel's, William J. Read, sometimes visited them and on one occasion asked her, *"and when are you going to begin thinking about music? I expect your father would have wished you to do something at it."*

Luckily her mother was out of the room and Avril was able to tell him that she had taught herself to play some of her father's music. In fact she had learnt to read music as naturally as reading books, but her mother had chosen to ignore the fact that she had any kind of musical gift.

"And I've written a song," she added. William J. Read listened as she sang it and was impressed, saying to her mother that she should be encouraged as she showed talent as a composer. Of course her mother would have ignored this advice but he was determined that the daughter of his friend should be given the opportunity to exercise her talent. It was through his perseverance that she was accepted at the age of 12, for a three-year scholarship at the Trinity College of Music.

Gordon Jacob and Alec Rowley were her tutors, and her first song, *Goodbye Butterfly* was published when she was 14.

Whilst at Trinity College Avril also took up dancing. She found it very hard work and the travelling involved, exhausting. Her mother, who was completely disinterested in anything her daughter did, showed no sympathy and piled on the chores for her when she returned home. This resulted in a diagnosis of heart strain and the doctor's insistence that she had complete rest for a few months.

During the First World War Hiawatha joined the French Red Cross as an ambulance driver. Avril continued her studies and also took part in wartime concerts where she played the piano, gave recitations and appeared in sketches. Without her brother at home she suddenly became of interest to her mother. Because of her age it was necessary that Jesse accompany her to concerts thus receiving a fee as manager/guardian. None of this, of course, was spent on Avril who was expected to buy her own clothes and pay her expenses from the payment she received herself.

However, because of these concerts she gained a certain monetary independence and was able to pay for singing lessons with Norman Notley. Singing had been recommended to her as being beneficial for her health.

On the return of her brother, after the war, the two became inseparable. Avril received affection from him that she had not experienced since the death of her father. She persuaded him to take up his music again and encouraged his gift for conducting. They performed together in a few concerts. The most successful took place at the Regal Cinema, Brighton. *"My brother conducted the orchestra accompanying me in the aria "Spring had come," from Hiawatha, and other music by our father."*

Promoters saw the novelty in this, two children performing their father's work and several more engagements followed. One of these was in Belfast and it was here that Avril met her first amour, a young man, Pat, who was a journalist. He was well educated, full of fun and true Irish humour. He was liked by both brother and sister and invited by Hiawatha, to visit them in England.

When he did come, Jesse seemed welcoming. Unfortunately after a few days Avril developed severe earache. Her mother showed no sympathy or noticed her daughter's pain and misery. Pat tried to understand her distress, but Jesse, interpreting their whisperings with suspicion, locked Avril in her bedroom for three days, during which time the pain in her ear became agonising. On the fourth day Pat left, promising to write. That evening the doctor was called. He diagnosed a severe abscess and asked how long it had caused her pain. *"I could scarcely believe mother's reply,"* wrote Avril. *"Turning to me she asked: "Why didn't you tell me you had ear-ache?" --- How could she possibly be so cruel?"*

Her misery was increased when no letters from Pat arrived. Of course he had written, and Jesse had collected and read them. After about six weeks she produced them. Avril knew they had been tampered with especially when Jesse laughingly quoted from one, to a friend, telling her that an Irish boy had written it in a letter to Gwen. He had written, *"Never wave a friend out of sight – it is unlucky."*

All this suffering and parental abuse culminated, a few months later, when Avril was pushed into the company of an elderly rake. Jesse knew that he was married and also that he was wealthy. To Avril's horror, one evening, he asked her to become his mistress, promising her a luxury flat and lovely clothes. Her response was to run, and when she reached home she told her mother and brother what had happened. Jesse looked at her blankly as if pretending that she knew nothing about it but it was obvious to Avril that her mother would have, without hesitation, sold her to this man, for money.

During her time at Trinity College she met John Barbarolli, a former student, who was at the beginning of his conducting career. In a letter to her, years later, he expressed his delight that the first work he conducted was her father's *Petite Suite de Concert*.

Her piano teacher was Agnes Winter who often despaired at Avril's work because it seemed to fluctuate between good and bad. Avril knew this was because of conditions at home but did not admit this to her teacher.

She loved playing Bach and Beethoven but at student concerts she always played pieces composed by her father.

However, at Miss Winter's request, she composed a piece of her own, an *Interlude*, that she played for a recital at the Aeolian Hall. She was then 14, and was thrilled to receive some very exciting press reports. *"Of no little interest and importance was a new Interlude by Gwendolen Coleridge-Taylor, distinguished daughter of a distinguished sire, a brilliant little affair well worthy of the attention of the few pianists who can bring themselves to avoid the beaten track."* (Excerpt from The Daily Telegraph.)

Just before her 17th birthday Avril became engaged to a flautist, Joseph Slater, who was 24. He had called at her house, on recommendation of friends, hoping that Avril would join him in giving recitals. Her mother had eventually agreed and the result was a series of concerts at the Public Hall, Croydon. Avril learnt much about the flute and wrote several pieces for flute and piano. The concerts were a success and the two became known as *"that musical pair."*

One day, whilst rehearsing, Joseph proposed. Of course Jesse, on hearing this, put on a frigid face. One minute she encouraged them, the next, did not. She met Joseph's parents several times but could not agree with any wedding arrangements that they suggested. Finally she announced that the engagement was off. A few weeks later, when Joseph called, hoping for reconciliation, she seemed to have changed her mind, but in effect she was planning something that would destroy their relationship forever.

Alone, with Avril she announced in a hostile voice, *"You must not marry this man, nor any man. It is my duty as your mother, to tell you that should you have a child you will become an invalid for life. If that happened you would become a great burden to this man. --- He would very soon tire of you and would seek happiness elsewhere. He is that type."*

She then secretly spoke to Joseph, who emerged white faced and announced that their engagement was over. Avril was devastated but in such fear of her mother and what she might do to her, that she was forced to accept this decision.

Eventually she did marry, a man called Harold Dashwood. Her father's music was played at the wedding and the cake decorated with motifs from Hiawatha. Avril was at last able to leave home and the couple moved into a flat in St. John's Wood, then later to a bungalow at Coulsdon in Surrey. When she found that she was to have a baby she became nervous and fearful, recalling her mother's words to her when she was courting Joseph.

She was right to beware of her mother's ability to once again disrupt her life. Jesse, in her usual dominant way arranged for her daughter to be cared for in an expensive nursing home for six weeks before her son Nigel was born, but to Avril's horror later sent all the bills for her to pay, in the same way as she had with her wedding expenses. This crippled Avril financially and as if this wasn't enough, her mother demanded £100 – as a gift.

To keep the peace, Avril gave it to her.

Her husband's prospects in the motor trade seemed to fluctuate badly and Avril became desperate. She tried to take up her career again but solving her household expenses became almost impossible. The Bank Manager was less than sympathetic, told her to demand the money back from her mother or sell up her home and move her family into one room.

It wasn't surprising that she became ill, decided to separate from her husband and moved out to live with friends.

It had been seven years since she had composed any music but she was able to rent a village hall for a few hours every day and thus start to pick up the pieces. It was there, in April, that she wrote her first work for orchestra. The title was *To April* and this inspiration spurred her on to change her name from Gwendolyn to Avril, thus psychologically trying to forget the horrors of her past life.

Its first performance was in a weekend concert, at Eastbourne during the summer season of 1929. It was to be played by the Municipal Orchestra and conducted by Captain Amers. He invited Avril to attend the final rehearsal on the morning of the concert and surprised her by stepping down from the rostrum and handing her the baton. "*I've never conducted in my life*," she explained but he wouldn't accept this and encouraged her to go ahead.

It was a life changing experience. She had discovered a longing to become a conductor, knew that she needed instruction, and sought the advice of Sir Henry Wood. He suggested that she accept offers to conduct as often as possible and arranged for her to learn stick technique from Ernest Read.

After her divorce she moved to an apartment in St. John's Wood and found herself in the centre of a musical community. Antonio Brosa, the violinist, lived two doors away, the composer Joseph Holbrooke lived in the next road, and Ernest Read just round the corner, very handy for her conducting lessons.

Through Sir Henry's recommendation Avril received invitations to conduct from a number of orchestras. She made her debut as a conductor in the Royal Albert Hall, in 1933, and was delighted to be asked by the Colonel of the Royal Marines to conduct *To April* and her father's *Othello Suite*. In this capacity she became the first female conductor of H.M.S. Royal Marine Band.

She was also frequently asked to be a guest conductor for the BBC Orchestra and the London Symphony Orchestra.

After the Second World War Avril married Bruce, an artistic friend.

They had both served in the R.A.F. and Avril had conducted a choir for him in Scotland. Together, in memory of her father, they started the Coleridge-Taylor Musical Society, the President being Sir Arnold Bax and the committee made up of well-known musicians.

The aim of the society was to give opportunities to British composers by presenting a new composition every season. From this the Coleridge-Taylor Symphony Orchestra was founded.

There was no Arts Council support or any financial help to pay for this, even though it was constantly requested by the committee and Avril became responsible for all the expenses of an orchestra numbering 80-90 players, the vast majority of them being professionals.

The conductor was David McCallum and many soloists appeared, including the pianists Clifford Curzon and Livia Rev, and Frank Sale from the Royal Opera Company.

The Society later became known as the New Era Concert Society, losing the Coleridge-Taylor name because of the inference that it may be an organisation for the family's gain.

The orchestra always played to capacity houses even in the Royal Albert Hall, but their expenses including taxation, fees and the hire of music, proved enormous.

Avril's husband, Bruce, worked as manager and secretary, but found it hard to cope under such adverse circumstances. They moved from the country to the outskirts of London, which was more ideal for their work, but the orchestra could not finance them both. Bruce was unable to find himself other work and thus contribute. Finally they drifted apart and divorced. Later he married again.

In May 1952, Avril travelled to South Africa on a concert tour. She was to conduct two concerts with the orchestra of the SABC (South African Broadcasting Corporation), in Johannesburg. To her surprise, when meeting the players for the first time, she found that her ex fiancé Joseph Slater was the leading flautist.

Before her departure she had agreed to meet Sir Arthur Bliss in London to go through the score of his *Violin Concerto* and *Theme and Cadenza* that were to receive their first performances on the tour.

Other concerts were organised with the Municipal Orchestras of Cape Town and Durban. Avril also took part in recitals and gave lectures. One lecture on *The Violin Concerto* by Sir Arthur Bliss was at the Houghton College for boys, in Natal.

In Durban the programmes included *Walton's Coronation March*, *Haydn Wood's Elizabeth of England* and *Josef Holbrooke's Tourmalin Suite,* as well as some of Avril's own compositions including the last movement of her *Piano Concerto.*

At Cape Town University she was asked to give a talk about her father – *My Father and his Music.* A violinist was provided to play her father's *Ballade in C minor.* Avril was nervous about doing this, fearing there may be some prejudice towards her, but nothing untoward happened and the audience was very appreciative. In South Africa her father was just a name on a list of composers and details of his life was not generally known or of concern to the majority of people.

Avril felt that she was there for her own worth and not because of the fame of her father. In fact she was treated as any travelling European and because of this assumed that she might be able to do some good, *" I felt even that I might bring a change, a little gleam of light, into the hearts of some black people because my own origins gave me particular understanding. --- I was to have a bitter lesson."*

She found Johannesburg a very busy, yet different place to live, the differences being the apartheid attitudes and the standard of living between black and white. When she landed, on that first day, she was hit by the immense heat from a cloudless sky that sparkled on the windows of the large number of skyscrapers. The city bustled. Cars crawled along the crowded roads in permanent traffic jams and she was informed that anybody using a pedestrian crossing at the wrong time, going against the lights was liable to an immediate fine.

She rented a furnished flat serviced by a *"flat boy"*. The owners of the building employed these boys for £8.00 a month and provided them with a room at the top of the house with a straw mattress to sleep on. They sent their money home to their families but rarely visited. Avril's "flat boy", John, during the time that she lived there, received news that his wife had given birth and knew that it would be a year old before he would see his child. *"It will be a big baby then,"* he told Avril, *"with long legs."*

She found this heart breaking and prepared a parcel of baby garments for him to send to his family. He was so excited by this and *" went on repeating his thanks, so that an unending flow of simple gratitude poured from his lips."*

Avril returned to England aware that the tour had been a success and that she had made many friends. She had gained a wealth of experience and certain organisations had promised her future employment. Thus her return to England was simply to sell her house and prepare herself for a new life.

Back in South Africa the work that she expected to be offered did not materialise. Somehow her origins had become known. A journal for which she had been contracted to submit articles, refused to pay her, saying that they had gone bankrupt. She obtained another job, in a records department, turned up on the first day and was told that the girl whose place she was to fill had decided not to leave.

Finally she was interviewed and offered the position of music teacher in a well-known girls school but a few days later received a telegram that said, *"Cancel all arrangements."* She found out that *"an English teacher on the staff had ruled out the suggestion of my being accepted owing to my father's colour."*

Friends began to shun her. An art student who she had helped to finance his journey to South Africa and with whom she sometimes met for coffee, thrust a note into her hand, one day, that said, *"I have been warned against meeting you, or even being seen speaking to you. Doubtless you will understand why."*

Avril became desperate. Weeks passed with little prospect of finding work. The worry and lack of food told on her health. Rescue came, at last, in the form of a doctor acquaintance, named Mark. During their initial friendship he had not known that Avril had Krio origins. It was only when he called and found her huddled in her flat, ill and desperate, that she eventually told him the whole story. Far from shunning her, he sympathised. Avril wrote, *"The remembrance of his gentle approach, his remarkable understanding and sympathy is something I shall always remember."*

She knew him to be a good doctor but programmed as all white South Africans were, to believe that the black natives would rise up against the whites. *"All South Africa,"* he said, *"lives in fear of such a rebellion."*

Mark travelled to Pretoria and spoke, on her behalf, to the High Commissioner for the United Kingdom. Two days later Avril was granted an appointment to see him. He was very sympathetic, yet the outcome was disappointing. He believed she had no option but to return home to England. If she didn't she could end up by being sent to prison.

She made her way back to Britain, poorer and wiser. She was sad at leaving her flat on the top of a hill situated in an avenue of beautiful Jacaranda trees. She would miss the magnificent scenery, the colourful sunsets, the music and laughter and sitting on the stoep in the evening listening to the crickets.

She had learned a hard lesson, had come up against humans and their prejudice, and realised the dignity and fortitude that her father had shown when shunned in the western world, for his colour.

As the daughter of a famous composer Avril was fortunate to be helped by people who knew and respected him, making it difficult, in a way, to create her own identity. In South Africa she had begun to feel that she was valued for her own accomplishments, but sadly the barrier of apartheid reared its impenetrable head and, even though only a quarter black, she had to accept the prejudice engendered by the white South African's towards the black.

However her connections with Africa were not totally severed. In 1957 she was commissioned to write a Ceremonial March to celebrate Ghana's Independence.

Amongst the 90 compositions to her name are large-scale orchestral works as well as keyboard and chamber music. Between 1917 and 1971 she wrote over 35 songs including the *Dreaming Water Lily* and *O'er all the Hilltops,* to words by Longfellow.

She also wrote a book, The Heritage of Samuel Coleridge-Taylor that was published by Dobson Books in 1979.

Nobody would wish for the childhood persecutions imposed on her by an uncaring mother but Avril overcame them, succeeded in her musical career with the help of benefactors, as her father had done, and became one of the most outstanding women conductors of her time, forming her own orchestra and choir, directing productions on stage and taking part in broadcasts.

She died at the age of 95, on the 21st December 1998 at Seaford, in East Sussex.

Compositions

Orchestral
To April, 1933.
Sussex Landscape, Op. 27. 1936
Ceremonial March 1957.

Chamber Music
Idylle for flute and piano Op. 21.
Impromptu for flute and piano. Op. 33.
A Lament for flute and piano. Op.31.
Over 18 more pieces for piano and organ.

Songs
Over 35 written between 1917 and 1971.These include :-
Goodbye Butterfly Op.1 1917.
Mister Sun. Op.2
Silver stars. Op. 3
Who Knows? Op. 4. 1922
April. Op.5.
The Dreaming Water Lily Op. 6. 1923.
The Rustling Grass. Op.7.
The Entranced Hour. Op. 8.
Regret. 1939.
Love's Philosophy
*O'er all the hillto*ps, 1957
I can face it. 1971
Nightfall Op.43.
Apple Blossom, Op. 44
Sleeping and Waking. Op.45

19. Gustav Holst, 1923.

20. Imogen Holst conducting at Dartington, 1942.

Chapter 8

Imogen Holst

1907 - 1984

"Composition was the area in which Imogen excelled as a student, and though her life was to take on many tasks essential to the vitality of the English musical scene in the mid- twentieth century, her talent for composition never left her, and indeed reached its fruition in the works of her last years. She spoke little of it, but was heard to remark on the publication of her String Quintet: "Ah! I feel like a real composer!"
Imogen Holst - A Life in Music edited by Christopher Grogan, Published to celebrate the 100th anniversary of her birth.

Imogen was born into music. She lived her life in its creation, as a player, dancer, teacher, composer and conductor.

She was the daughter of Gustav Holst, a composer of rising fame and had every opportunity, as a woman in the 20th century, to follow her own ambitions.

The progress of her musical career was, however, greatly influenced by two men who were important in her life, her father, Gustav, and Benjamin Britten, a composer who she admired above any other and for whom she felt privileged to work. For over 12 years she was musical assistant to Britten and artistic director of the Aldeburgh Festival.

In 1964 she left Aldeburgh to concentrate on editing her father's works, with Colin Matthews. These were published as *A Thematic Catalogue of Gustav Holst's Music*, in 1974.

It was during the latter part of her life, after the completion of this work, and her departure from Aldeburgh, that most of her finest music was composed, including, as previously mentioned, her most well known *String Quintet* of 1982.

Imogen trained at the Royal College of Music, where, as a student, her conducting attracted attention. A Daily Telegraph critic wrote, *" No woman has yet managed to establish a secure tenure of the conductor's platform, so that Imogen Holst may prove the first of her sex to do this."*

She won several scholarships at the College, including the Octavia Travelling Scholarship. She was passionate about folk music, and considered to be an unconventional yet outstanding teacher.

Rosamund Strode, one of her students wrote, *"She was one of the world's great teachers and was able to communicate to all who met her a knowledge and love of music and exactly what she required from her players and singers."*

She had many research interests and gave lectures at the University of East Anglia. In 1966, for the Aldeburgh Festival, she lectured on the theme, *What is Musical History?* In the audience was Joyce Grenfell who later wrote to a friend, *"It was utterly fascinating and absolutely first class. She came on trippingly, head down. Not a trace of powder or lipstick on that fifteenth century head painted on wood. A pale beige dress blending in with face and hair. Almost invisible really. And then she began. It was a miracle of erudition, simplicity, interest, passion and wit. Haven't enjoyed anything more during the whole festival."*

Imogen Claire Holst was born on 12th April, 1907 at 31 Grena Road, Richmond. Her father was the composer, Gustav Holst, her mother, Isobel Harrison. Isobel had met Gustav when she joined the Socialist Choir, as a soprano, a choir that he conducted.

Gustav, who was going through his Indian phase, wanted to call her *Sita* (The daughter of the Earth), but Isobel persuaded him against this as she had fair hair with bright blue eyes and an Indian name seemed unsuitable.

After his initial joy at Imogen's arrival Gustav, a man who needed peace and solitude in which to compose, found the noise and upheaval of a new baby more than he could cope with. She appeared to howl all day, and, to the singer Maja Kjöhler, who lived nearby, he wrote, *"Imogen is practising coloratura – the sort that foghorns usually perform – and my brain feels pulpy whenever she lets fly."*

Fortunately an aunt of his, who ran a small school loaned them a house, No. 10 The Terrace, Barnes. Gustav was able to set up a music room on the top floor, *"a room that one didn't go into,"* wrote Imogen, whilst the family lived below.

Gustav was born Gustavus Theodore von Holst on the 21st September 1874, in a small house in Pittville Terrace, Cheltenham. His parents were Adolph and Clara von Holst.

The Holst's were a musical family. Matthias, Gustav's great grandfather, was of Swedish origin, a composer of little fame, but a notable harp player. His musical life led him to Riga in Latvia and St. Petersburg in Russia, where he taught the harp to the Imperial Family. His political opinions however were unwelcome and he was forced to escape, with his Russian wife and small son Gustavus Valentine, to England.

Gustavus Valentine was also a composer and pianist. He married an English woman and settled in Cheltenham as a teacher.

He had two sons, Gustavus Matthias, who was a precociously brilliant pianist, and Adolph. Gustavus Matthias delighted in entrancing the young ladies of Cheltenham, led a scandalous life, and was forced to seek employment in Glasgow, from which he was told never to return.

Adolph was also a brilliant pianist. He remained in Cheltenham, led a busy life giving orchestral concerts at the Rotunda, taught a large number of piano pupils and was organist and choirmaster at All Saints' Church, Pittville.

In 1872, he married one of his pupils, Clara Lediard, daughter of a solicitor. Her family disapproved of her marrying a musician even though he taught some of the elite families in Cheltenham. Clara was a gentle young woman but lacked vitality, and died in 1882, when Gustav was only eight and his brother, Emil, six.

Adolph's sister, Nina moved in to look after the two boys. She was also a keen pianist but not much use around the house. She helped Gustav with his practicing but failed to spot that his eyesight was poor and that his asthma caused breathing problems so that he had to rest halfway up the stairs instead of climbing straight to the top.

He loved practicing the piano, but hated the violin. His brother Emil played tricks on him by putting the clock back when he was doing his bowing exercises.

Adolph remarried in 1885. His new wife was Mary Thorley Stone who bore two more sons, Matthias Ralph and Evelyn Thorley.

Gustav was educated at Cheltenham Grammar School for boys, then, in 1893 left home for London as a student at the Royal College of Music.

He was tutored in composition by Stanford, took up the trombone because of neuritis in his right hand, lived frugally in lodgings without a piano, did not drink or smoke and became a vegetarian resulting in a worsening of his eyesight. He was considered to be single-minded, sincere but a little naïve, was reclusive by nature but also interested in people and had an enormous laugh that appeared to be the most robust thing about him.

To eke out his college grant he played trombone on Brighton pier during the holidays.

At the college he met Ralph Vaughan Williams, who became a lifelong friend. He was also influenced by Socialism and, as previously mentioned, conducted the Socialist choir thus meeting Isobel, his wife. He was only 22 and, with her golden hair and blue eyes, thought her the most beautiful person he had ever met.

She soon took him in hand encouraging him to shave off his beard, eat food that benefited his eyesight and strengthened his hand, and invited him to her house where he enjoyed a family atmosphere that he had never previously known. He wrote her a love song every week and worked tirelessly to earn more money.

Gustav played the organ in several churches and the trombone in orchestras, when he could. He was ever conscious of the monetary pressure that came from home. His father had broken his wrist and could no longer play the piano. There were two small half-brothers to care for, and his brother Emil had runaway to go on the stage and often wrote home asking for money, in one instance to buy a dress suit for a part he was to play. He eventually moved to America and became a Hollywood actor using the name Ernest Cossart.

In the autumn of 1898 Gustav was offered an appointment of first trombone in the Carl Rosa Opera Company. Although he had composed from the age of 12 he found little time to do so whilst he was touring. However in 1902 his *Cotswolds Symphony*, his most ambitious and first mature work had its first performance at the Winter Gardens at Bournemouth.

In the summer of 1901 he married Isobel. On the death of his father he inherited a small legacy and in 1903 he spent it all on a belated honeymoon, to Berlin.

On his return he began a career as a teacher at the James Allen Girls' School at Dulwich. In 1905 he was appointed Director of Music at St. Paul's Girls School in Hammersmith and in 1907 Musical Director at the Morley College for Working Men and Women. He continued in these latter two positions until his death.

As Imogen grew up in the house in Barnes, music became part of her life. Upstairs, in his music room Gustav composed in isolation, but downstairs he was always a devoted father. Imogen wrote, *"I first got to know my father as someone who played tunes on the piano for me to dance to. --- By the time I was four he was teaching me to sing folk songs – a difficult business when one had a lisp and couldn't pronounce the letter "R". I can still remember struggling with, "Ath I wath going to Shtwarbuwy Fair."*

Her parents, realising her enthusiasm, sent her to dance classes before she started school. When she was four she made her first public appearance as a toadstool wearing a large-brimmed hat.

In 1912, at the age of five, she started at the Froebel Demonstration School in Colet Gardens. *"My two years there were an enchanted time. I remember no punishment, no rows, no squabbles ---- in this happy and harmonious paradise we sang, we painted, we made cardboard models, we stuck chestnut buds in jam jars, we acted Hiawatha, we became knights with shields and swords, we kept animals."*

In 1915 she contracted typhoid and was taken to a cottage in Monk Street, Thaxted, to recuperate. It was a quiet, peaceful place, ideal for her long convalescence and a place where her father was able to work on his *Planets Suite*.

During the years of the First World War people were often suspicious of Gustav because of his name so he decided to change it and leave out the "von", discovering, in the process, that he had no right to the prefix anyway, it had been added by an ancestor to improve the image of his family.

He had been turned down for war service due to his bad eyesight, lungs and digestion, but he was appointed YMCA Musical Organiser for the troops in the Eastern Mediterranean. By the time he actually left to take up this appointment the war was nearly over. However he did spend time in Greece and Turkey teaching music to troops who welcomed a change in their daily routine.

In 1917 Imogen became a boarder at Eothen, a small private school near Caterham, Surrey. She began violin lessons and started to compose. Isobel sent many of her compositions to Gustav, while he was away.

At that time Imogen's sights were set on becoming a dancer. When she left Eothen at Christmas 1920 she hoped to get a place at the Ginner-Mawer School of Dance and Drama, but she was rejected on health grounds and advised to spend time in the open air. Instead, in September she started at St. Paul's Girls School, where her father was Director of Music.

Once again the family moved, this time to 32 Gunterstone Road, Baron's Court that would be their home until Imogen left school in 1925.

When she was 16 she won the Alice Lupton Prize for music, at St. Paul's and also became a member of the English Folk Dance Society. In the summer holidays she attended the Society's Summer School at Aldeburgh where she first heard Cecil Sharp play the piano.

As previously mentioned, her father had given up all ideas of becoming a concert pianist due to severe neuritis in his right arm and ironically a similar fate befell Imogen. In 1924 she had to receive treatment for phlebitis in her left arm thus hampering her own ambitions as a pianist.

In September 1924 Gustav celebrated his 50th birthday. His popularity was growing due to the success of *The Planets Suite*. In 1925 the family moved from Thaxted to Brook End, Dunmow, in Essex. The house was half-timbered with a separate building on the side that was converted into a music room for Gustav.

Imogen left school in July 1925 with the intention of gaining a place at the Royal College of Music. She worked hard in order to give herself the best chance of success. She had composition lessons from Herbert Howells and studied piano with Adine O'Neill, a concert pianist who had been one of the last pupils of Clara Schumann. She no longer played the violin but had taken up the organ and French horn instead. She had learnt how to train a choir and conduct an orchestra, gaining valuable knowledge as to writing for the various instruments.

She gained a place at the RCM in the autumn of 1926, receiving considerable attention from the press and musical profession due to her father's fame. However she was perfectly capable of holding her own, and did not need to trade on his success. She admitted, however, that bearing his name was useful, especially when travelling abroad when he would write notes of introduction for her to his Continental friends and colleagues. Gustav had always been an avid rambler and great traveller.

At the College Imogen studied composition with George Dyson, piano with Kathleen Long and conducting with William H. Reed, who had been leader of the London Symphony Orchestra and was a great friend of Edward Elgar. Vaughan Williams taught her harmony and counterpoint. She also enjoyed ballet classes with Penelope Spencer and continued her involvement with the English Folk Dancing Society.

Composition, however occupied a large portion of her time. She completed two orchestral suites, along with a *Mass in A minor* that became one of the longest works in her whole career and earned her the comment of *"Good, I like it,"* from Herbert Howells. In May she entered for an Open Scholarship for Composition and was thrilled to find that she had won. This gave her £60 per annum for three years.

Having won this competition, composing became her primary study with piano and conducting second.

In 1928 she moved into a bed-sitting room of her own at 42 Craven Road, on the north side of Kensington Gardens. Her days were filled with composing chamber music and solo instrumental works, along with dancing in public performances, and conducting. During the holidays she travelled abroad, sometimes with a dance group and attended the English Folk Dance Society's Summer School.

In October she was awarded the Cobbett Prize for composition for *A Phantasy String Quartet.* This was performed for the first time in February 1929 at an RCM College Chamber Concert. In December 1928 she spent her prize of 15 guineas on a holiday to the Swiss Alps with two friends.

She was also awarded the Morley Scholarship for the best all round student. This paid her College fees and gave her an annual sum of £52 10s a year, which was later renewed for another year.

At the conclusion of her time at the RCM she left to travel Europe on her Octavia Travel Scholarship absorbing the musical ethos of Sweden, Denmark, Germany, Austria and Italy.

When she returned in 1931 she began to earn her living as a freelance musician. All hope of being a concert pianist had been dashed due to the phlebitis in her left arm. One of her first occupations was to give a talk about her travels abroad to the Society of Women Musicians at their annual Conference. A newspaper report commented that, *"it engaged its audience by saying wise things in a witty way.*" This was to be a characteristic of her lectures in the years to come.

For a short while she became accompanist for Citizen House, Bath, a theatrical venture providing training in drama and all other production work in the theatre. However she found the duties onerous, and resigned.

She then decided to take over the role of Jane Joseph, her father's musical confidante, who had died in 1929, and work with him, for the last few years of his life, enjoying his successes and pacifying him when things did not go so well.

In 1932 she joined the staff of the English Folk Dance Society where her enthusiasm and organisational skills were greatly appreciated, as were her talents as an accompanist and conductor.

It was at this time that the phlebitis in her arm began to seriously trouble her. Gustav discussed her condition with Dr. Donald Guy, a consultant physician who suggested that an operation might help, but not cure.

Because there was no guarantee of success Imogen declined to have the operation. Gustav felt this as a bitter blow particularly as he had also had to forego his aspirations of being a concert pianist for similar reasons.

Following in her father's footsteps she diversified into teaching for which she had a remarkable gift, and worked over the next ten years with a great many amateur musicians.

She also made her mark with her *Morris Suite*, an arrangement for orchestra of four dance tunes collected by Cecil Sharp. This was performed by the BBC Theatre Orchestra at Cecil Sharp House to celebrate the English Folk Dance Society's 21st Anniversary.

In February 1933 she became the first woman to conduct a brass band at a public concert. The band was St. Stephen's Brass Band based in Carlisle. Her father, who organised the concert, remembered that she had written the suite *The Unfortunate Traveller*, for a brass band at the RCM, knew that it had only been performed as an arrangement for a String Orchestra and added it to the band's programme.

Also that year she became music teacher at Eothen School,

Caterham, where she had once been a pupil and where her old Headmistress, Miss Pye still *ruled*. Here she taught composition, piano and singing and gave concerts, often attended by Vaughan Williams who lived nearby. Daphne Hereward, one of her pupil's wrote, *"Vaughan Williams was not allowed to have Miss Pye's chair because he was very fat and the chair might have collapsed."*

Her pupils found her unconventional teaching methods exciting. One commented, *"She never walked, she danced ---."* Christopher Grogan writes, *"Her conducting was remembered as infectious and her singing classes as sheer joy and there can be no doubt that she was highly successful in enthusing her pupils and firing their musical imaginations."*

To add to her income she accepted a teaching post at Roedean School, in Sussex, where she taught about twenty piano pupils as well as aural training classes. She stayed overnight for part of the week, earned £50.00 a term, but found the staff unwilling to accept any changes that she wanted to make, especially in the introduction of European music. In 1935, after two years, she resigned.

From 1933 her father's health began to deteriorate. On 23rd May 1934 he was taken into hospital to have an ulcer removed. The operation was a success but, sadly, he died of heart failure, two days later.

On 28th May Gustav was cremated at Golders Green and then on the 24th June his ashes were interred in Chichester Cathedral. Bishop George Bell gave the memorial ovation, and Vaughan Williams conducted a massed choir in a selection of Gustav's work along with his own, and some written by the 16th century composer Thomas Weelkes who was also buried in the Cathedral.

In September 2009 a week of concerts was held at the cathedral in memory of Holst and a plaque unveiled with a text from the *Hymn of Jesus* that read, *"The heavenly spheres make music for us."*

Immediately following his death obituaries and commemorative articles were featured in national newspapers and the musical press, but after these declined, so did the playing of his music.

Vaughan Williams and Adrian Boult did their utmost to keep it in the public's mind but it was Imogen who finally decided to dedicate her life in preserving her father's legacy.

Gustav had left a small estate to be shared between his wife and daughter. Imogen took little of it for herself feeling that her mother's needs were greater as Isobel was beginning to suffer from arthritis.

Her first task was to finish *The Song of Solomon*, music that Gustav had begun writing for a Hollywood pageant. She submitted it on the 30th August but the project was abandoned and the score not returned.

During the next few years she arranged concerts, gave lectures and saw some of her own compositions published and performed. On 15th November 1935 she conducted her *Concerto for Violin and String Orchestra*, based on Irish tunes and during 1936 arranged the music for some major events, one being the National Festival of English Folk Dance and Song that took place at the Royal Albert Hall.

She was asked to be an adjudicator at the Leith Hill Music Festival with Vaughan Williams, wrote new songs for the Society of Women Musicians 25th Anniversary and began work with the Dolmetsch family on music for recorder groups, to be published by Schott's.

She was also commissioned, with Gordon Jacob, to do arrangements of country dances to be recorded by Columbia to celebrate King George VI Coronation.

Along with teaching, these all helped to boost her income and she was able to move into a new flat at 54 Ormonde Terrace, Primrose Hill.

The preserving of her father's legacy was, however her prime concern. With Vaughan Williams and other musicians she campaigned for a new soundproofed music room at Morley College. Raising the money, £1,100, took 18 months. Queen Mary opened the building, designed by Edward Maufe, on the 6th March 1937.

Imogen also became her father's biographer. The book,

Gustav Holst, published by Oxford University Press in 1938, was rapturously received by both the musical world and the Press. Edward Rubbra in the Monthly Musical Record of November 1938 wrote, *"It is usually perilous for a daughter to take it upon herself to be her father's biographer. --- Imogen Holst has, however, inherited from her father not a little of his sense of proportion, so that her biography is at once intimate and objective."*

Following this publication, Imogen found herself questioning what she wanted to be and do. She decided to give up her connections with amateur associations. Her reputation had been increasing. She did not (without any sense of pride) want her future career to be hindered. Through her father's fame she had been in contact with many famous names in music and literature and she felt that it was time to prove herself as one of them. It took her almost a decade to finally break away from work with amateurs.

At Easter 1939 she resigned from her post at Eothen and travelled to Switzerland but was forced to return hurriedly reaching home only two days before the Second World War broke out. During the war she worked for the Bloomsbury house Refugee Committee, led by Vaughan Williams. The objective was to aid the release, from internment, of musicians who had escaped from Austria and Germany.

She also became one of six "Music travellers" for the Pilgrim's Trust, organising musical activities for civilians, in rural areas. Edward Harkness, an American philanthropist had founded the Trust in 1930 as acknowledgement of Britain's efforts in the 1914-18 war, and endowed it with two million pounds. The money was to be used for the country's cultural needs. When the Second World War broke out Dr. Thomas Jones, the Trust's Secretary decided to use some of the money to keep alive traditions and culture. The venture had the backing of the Government,

"This country is supposed to be fighting for civilization and democracy and if these things mean anything they mean a way of life where people have liberty and opportunity to pursue the things of peace." Quote by the Board of Education.

In this role Imogen was assigned to the West of England. She found the diversity of activities that she experienced, exciting. These ranged from singsongs at an evacuee hostel for mothers and babies, to attending a string orchestra practice in an ironmonger's shop led by the village postman.

Most exciting for her was the discovery of folk songs in Somerset, sung in their own traditional way.

The job was physically taxing and after two and a half years she resigned, having become ill with exhaustion. However she had accomplished a great deal, stimulated and kept alive many musical organisations. Later she wrote, *"There were never any song books and seldom any pianos, so I soon found that the best way of getting people to enjoy themselves was to teach them easy accumulative folk songs such as " My name is Jack Jintle" where the tunes went with a swing and the words were simple enough to pick up by ear."*

It was the lack of written material that encouraged her, much later, in 1957, to publish a volume of songs for female voices, for the Women's Institute, called *Singing for Pleasure.*

During this period her composing had greatly slowed down and she only wrote music relating to her work as a *travelle*r, for example arranging carols for female voices and suites for recorder trios.

One of these suites was *The Deddington Suite,* written for Marjorie Wise. Marjorie was headmistress of a school in Dagenham that had been evacuated to Deddington, Oxfordshire. Imogen had previously met Marjorie at Cecil Sharp House and had, in 1938 been introduced, by her, to Leonard and Dorothy Elmhirst of Dartington Hall, near Totnes, Devon, who were hoping to create an ideal community influenced by Leonard's work in rural India and in sympathy with the Arts and Crafts movement of William Morris. William Morris had been a textile-designer and important figure in the emergence of Socialism, of which both Imogen and her father had sympathies.

Four years later the Elmhirsts' invited her to stay at the Hall permanently whilst she worked in Devon and Cornwall. It was there, towards the end of her time as a traveller that Imogen had the inspiration to create an Arts Centre in this wonderful setting where *"music and the other arts could be a living experience for the locality."* The building up of this Arts Centre was to dominate her life for the next eight years.

Imogen organised a one-year course for young people who wished to become leaders in the local community, either in singing or leading an orchestra. The course would include sight-reading, transposing, elementary conducting, harmony, orchestration and transcribing music for singers or players. Because of conscription the course started with four 16 year olds, one boy and three girls.

Open evenings brought in land girls in muddy boots, evacuee school teachers who worked with children evacuated to Dartington Hall, and wounded American airmen, convalescing in the area. All these enthusiasts came to be taught singing and playing, and an orchestra was built up of about 60 players hardly any of whom could play well.

Imogen was inspired to rejuvenate her composing, both for the needs of the students and for herself. As a result, 300 people subscribed funds to pay for a London concert that she would conduct and that would be compiled of her works alone. This took place in July 1942, at the Wigmore Hall and included first performances of the *Serenade, Suite for String Orchestra*, and *Three Psalms*.

The reviews were good and did much to renew her faith in herself as a composer.

She felt revitalised in the peace of Dartington. Now in her mid thirties she was well travelled, adaptable, an experienced lecturer and had a great gift for encouraging students in musical pursuits. She proved a loyal friend but was reclusive about her private life. She had chosen to remain unmarried, music was her fulfilment, but she was, at times, lonely, even though the work at Dartington suited her perfectly and she was genuinely happy.

" *- when it is one's job and one is allowed to choose the music one wants to do, those worries are not worries – they are part* *of living. The exhaustion at the end of the day is not desperate exhaustion but is really the exhilaration at the end of a lovely day of lovely music.*"

She was immensely proud of her orchestra, of the students that passed their exams, of her choir and emerging soloists that culminated in a performance of Bach's B minor Mass in July 1950 to celebrate the 200th anniversary of Bach's death.

Another of her achievements was in encouraging the formation of the Amadeus String Quartet. Through her war work with escaped Jews from Germany and Austria she had invited Norbert Brainin, a beautiful violin player, to Dartington and encouraged him to set up the Quartet, underwriting their first performance in the Wigmore Hall, on 10th January 1948.

In 1947, now that the music department at Dartington had grown and become established she began to realise that her unorthodox methods of teaching needed to conform more to national standards and syllabuses.

She had become restless and, as previously mentioned desired to break away from her association with amateurs believing that "*there is so much other music still to explore.*"

Many musicians had visited and played at Dartington, including Benjamin Britten and Peter Pears. Imogen was immediately struck by the music written by Britten, judging his compositions as superb matches to those of Baroque and Renaissance masters whose music she greatly admired, as had her father.

Their first visit to Dartington had been in October 1943. They were both conscientious objectors and had worked, during the war, travelling the country giving concerts for the Council for the Encouragement of Music and the Arts (CEMA).

Over the next few years they gave regular recitals at Dartington. A mutual respect built up between Imogen and Benjamin Britten, and she began to take on various tasks for him. At this time his fame was growing through his two operas, *Peter Grimes* and *The Rape of Lucretia*.

Britten was planning to start a new opera company, the English Opera Group and it almost seemed that it might open at

Dartington in 1946, but the final (more permanent) venue chosen was Aldeburgh, where the first festival took place in 1948.

In 1950 Imogen decided to leave Dartington, giving a year's notice. She had been expanding her range of musical work by giving lectures at courses and at various Summer Schools. She also attended the inaugural Festival at Aldeburgh, was impressed with the surroundings and atmosphere and became determined to return the next year.

Britten had commissioned her to write a piece for female voices for the following year's Aldeburgh Festival. Based on poems by John Keats she wrote a song cycle of six songs, *Welcome Joy and Welcome Sorrow* that Britten and Pears found quite beautiful. She was also thrilled to be invited, the following June, to conduct the performance.

Having decided to leave Dartington she took a break for two months, and travelled to India in the winter of 1950/51. The trip, arranged by Leonard Elmhirst was to Santiniketan University in Western Bengal.

Having worked on folk music for the last 25 years she was keen to explore Indian music, as her father had in earlier years, and study the links between this culture and that of the Western world.

Although she appreciated the colourful creatures and flowers she also saw the overcrowding and poverty in Calcutta. These memories remained vividly in her mind, as did the grace and friendliness of the people she met.

When she returned to Dartington she wrote an arrangement for recorders, *Ten Indian Folk Tunes from the Hill Villages of the Punjab* from tunes that she had collected. *"The recorder is the right instrument for bridging the gap between eastern and western folk music, for Indians play home-made bamboo flutes. ---There is a welcome flexibility of intonation in the recorder which suits the Indian scales."*

In 1951 her book, *The Music of Gustav Holst,* was published by Oxford University Press. In her opinion her father had spent too much time teaching, and had not fulfilled his dream of seeing a Renaissance of music in England. He had been, as John the Baptist, clearing a path for the arrival of a greater composer. In her eyes this person was Benjamin Britten, to whom the book was dedicated.

Britten was aware of the pedestal on which she had placed him and was deeply honoured. A great bond of affection and respect was building up between them. Peter Pears, whilst working on a teaching assignment at Dartington, attended a class where her students were studying a Bach Chorale and was greatly impressed. He wrote to Britten, *"She is quite brilliant, - revealing, exciting. ------We have got to use Imo in the biggest way – as editor, trainer, as teacher – she is most impressive."*

When her successor, John Clements, was appointed Imogen left Dartington. She had no clear plans for employment and travelled to Europe, spending time in Paris and Venice, studying early chants and mediaeval polyphonic music.

On her return she took on freelance and copying work for Britten and helped with the correcting of the vocal score of *Billy Budd*. In April 1952 she stayed at Crag House, Britten's seafront house in Aldeburgh to work on the orchestration of his *Rejoice in the Lamb*, for the next years festival. She was thrilled to be doing this for him and he appreciated her professional efficiency, *"which amounts to genius."*

Then came the request that was to fulfil Imogen's dream, *"– next year --- will you count yourself as definitely engaged in the preparations and running of Aldeburgh Festivals."* Pleased to accept this invitation she moved to Aldeburgh on the 29th September 1952, never guessing that she would live there for the rest of her life.

During the first 18 months she kept a diary, writing each evening her memories of the day. Her complex personality is shown in this diary, along with her loyalty to friends and dedication to music. Her life was frugal. She was always anxious about money. She tried to write little about herself and mostly about her interaction with Britten, for whom she felt privileged to work. Her own life as a composer came to a standstill for these first few years.

She viewed Britten as nearly perfect and was extremely critical of herself. There is little doubt that she greatly missed her father and saw him as some kind of surrogate. Yet her admiration for his talent, youthfulness and athleticism, confirmed by her blushes at any praise he gave her, could possibly be assumed otherwise. However he was six years her junior and lived in a homosexual relationship with Peter Pears. Eventually her friendship became more maternal, (Britten also missed his mother as Imogen did her father), and she often assisted in mundane tasks such as packing his suitcases and doing his washing up.

However, the working relationship between them was built on mutual respect. They were both dedicated to music, hard working, clear thinking and purposeful, especially with plans for a music school and new theatre in Aldeburgh.

She settled into a bed-sitting room in Brown Acres that had once been the vicarage. Britten was, at that time, writing his opera *Gloriana* to be performed at Covent Garden as part of the celebrations taking place during the Coronation year of Queen Elizabeth II.

Imogen immediately immersed herself in the music of the town and was welcomed as a member of the newly formed Aldeburgh Music Club currently working on Purcell's *Timon of Athens*.

She wasted no time in beginning work for the annual Festival that took 11 months each year in planning. Her experience, musically, at Dartington stood her in good stead for the variety of work expected of her, especially as a conductor of choirs and orchestras, both professional and amateur. It was during this first year that she became recognised as a conductor especially when Britten invited her to conduct part of the Coronation concert in 1953. This was followed, the next year, by the acclamation she received for her interpretation of *Bach's St. John's Passion*.

Her conducting was distinctive and individual owing much to her time as a dancer. In 1957, the author Ronald Blythe wrote, *"Imogen Holst is the only conductor I have seen who appears to be "audience free." She is a suppliant at the rostrum. Do it for me, she seems to say – and of course, they do!"*

Her weekly routine consisted of weekdays at Aldeburgh and weekends in London. In London she worked with her newly formed, mostly professional choir, later called the Purcell Singers.

Obviously earning enough money on which to live was a priority. Britten asked her to help in the writing and preparation of his scores, she also taught pupils to play the piano and moved outside the confines of Aldeburgh to conduct musical groups and choirs.

Her life was exacting involving conducting, arranging concerts, necessary work for the Festival and endless copying out of orchestral parts as well as constantly seeking opportunities for promoting her father's works. By 1955 there was definite interest in his favour. Recording of *The Planets Suite* were selling well and *The Hymn of Jesus, The Perfect Fool and St.Paul's Suite* were also available on record.

In 1956 Britten and Pears went on an extensive far eastern trip having confidence that Imogen would take over the planning of the Festival with her gift of musicianship and organisational skills. She chose her friend, George Bell, Bishop of Chichester to preach at the Festival Service, conducted Handel's oratorio, *Samson*, in the opening concert and the Purcell Singers in their first concert for the Festival. She also brought together a choir of 230 children from East Sussex schools to give a concert of folk music along with items by Purcell, Handel, Holst and Britten.

In 1957 Imogen turned 50, the same year in which *Singing for Pleasure* was published for The Women's Institute.

Ronald Blythe wrote about her for the readers of *The Lady* magazine.

"At fifty there are scarcely enough hours in her day. She works in a tall, narrow-roomed flat perched up high amongst the roofs of Aldeburgh. ---- It is to this demure eyrie that she has brought her collection of rare scores and texts, her wit and charm, and her unique gifts.

Watching her as she works steadily on the latest pages sent over from Britten's study across the street, one feels certain that here, at least, is an artist where she was intended to be."

Imogen chose this year to expand her dedication to early English music by organising late night concerts in Aldeburgh Parish Church. These were surprisingly popular and continued until 1971. She also developed the concept of "themed" concerts beginning that year with a single concert to celebrate the quatercentenary of Thomas Morley.

She was always helpful to young composers who arrived at the Festival. Into this category came Malcolm Williamson, who she invited to a picnic lunch. It was a generous spread. They ate and discussed choral music. It was only later that Williamson discovered that she had given extra music lessons that morning to pay for it.

In 1957/8 she was able to assist Britten in his creation of *Noye's Fludde*, a project close to her heart because it involved a choir of schoolchildren.

By 1959 her workload was heavy. As an organiser she proved diligent and successful. However, her relationship with Britten was becoming shaky. He was finding her difficult to get along with and had become tired of her "disciple at his feet" attitude. He was working on his new opera, *A Midsummer Night's Dream* and wrote to Pears after a session, *"Imo good, but pretty wild – I'm doing my best to keep my temper!"* Five days later he wrote again, *"Imo panics" -- as "ff staccato".*

In February, halfway through the work on the vocal score for this opera Imogen was rushed into hospital with suspected appendicitis. After tests an ovarian cyst was diagnosed. This resulted in an operation and the instruction to her of not returning to work for six weeks.

She travelled to Dartington to recuperate, then, after visiting her mother, returned to Aldeburgh. The work on the opera score had been taken over by Martin Penny and in her absence Britten's attitude towards her had definitely changed. At times he found her exasperating and tended to mock her slightly, especially when she frequently referred to her "gynaecological operation."

As a result of her illness Imogen's participation in the 1960 Festival was greatly reduced. She lived in Spartan conditions, with very little money. She gave all the returns from the recordings of her father's increasingly popular works to her mother. Because of the tensions with Britten she decided to show her assertion and chase up any payment that he still owed her.

She eked out her money by doing arrangements and writing texts. With less work from Britten she undertook to write a book entitled *Tune*, commissioned by Geoffrey Faber. It was published in 1961 and displayed a refreshing tone and considerable humour that captivated the reader. It was based on Imogen's observations on the development of music and included references from traditional and contemporary music as well as early Renaissance and Baroque. Her reputation soared due to this publication and she was asked by the Arts Council of Great Britain to join their music panel.

She was, however still sought out by Britten, and helped to copy the score of his *War Requiem* that was performed in Coventry on 30th May 1962. It was to commemorate the consecration of the new cathedral designed to link with the ruins of the old, that had been bombed during the war.

Also in 1962 she moved into a new bungalow in Church Walk and started to renovate her lapsed composing career by accepting several commissions.

In 1963 she was proud to unveil a plaque to her father's memory at No.10 The Terrace, Barnes. This acknowledged that he was now considered to be a major figure in 20th century music. It was at this point that Imogen began to conceive new plans for securing his legacy and reputation. These plans began to dominate her thoughts and activities even to the extent of overshadowing her work for Britten.

Thus it was that in 1964 she decided to give up working full time for him and the Festival. She had become a sought after composer, writer and speaker in her own right. Many opportunities were being offered to her. Along with these was her desire to develop her father's musical estate. Foremost in her mind was the centenary of her father's birth in 1974. Although ten years ahead she planned to locate, and catalogue his manuscripts, encourage further performances of his music and put his affairs on a solid footing.

Some of her own compositions were also becoming re-established. *The String Trio No. 2* gained a second London performance on 15th July 1964.

Although her devotion to Britten remained, she had begun to realise that their working relationship was coming to an end. His standards were high. She felt she had let him down during his work on a *Midsummer Night's Dream*. She was aware that he found her complete devotion claustrophobic and by making her own decision to leave she held his affection and regard and they remained good friends for the rest of his life.

Now moving on to this new phase of her working life Imogen appointed a part-time secretary, Helen Lilley, and began the huge task of identifying and cataloguing her father's manuscripts.

She also began, once more, to compose. She wrote *As Laurel Leaves that Cease not to be Green* for The Purcell Consort, an ensemble of six voices who were an offshoot of the Purcell Singers. They performed this at the Wigmore Hall, in March 1965. She was asked to talk about her father and childhood for Woman's Hour. Her music was included in a programme by women composers at the Commonwealth Institute, and Faber issued a publication that she had written about Bach, in their *Great Composers* series.

Her days were busy writing commissioned work, lecturing on East Anglian composers at the University, conducting the Purcell Singers and doing recordings of some of her father's works.

Ursula Vaughan Williams, widow of Ralph, interviewed her for the purpose of writing a piece for the Performing Right Society. The article provided a portrait of Imogen showing her independent spirit and exhaustive lifestyle.

"Imogen Holst is a slight, fair-haired figure, usually armed with masses of work to do in trains or other unlikely places, finding time to seem to be in at least three places at once and to write at least three books at a time. She loves walking and rejoices in the cold winds of her beloved East Anglia. ----- Professionals and amateurs, past and present, have all a part in her being, and,

perhaps because this is so, she has the power of making each of them appreciate the place and value of the other."

In 1966 a new company, G. & I. Holst was established. This company, set up by Caplan and Leslie Periton, Britten's legal advisors superseded the old less well- established company. This was a necessary move due to the increased interest and income derived from her father's growing popularity. However Imogen still lived frugally and channelled most of the money to the care of her mother.

She did, however, allow herself some luxuries. Sitting in a restaurant, one day, with Maureen Graham, manager of the Purcell Singers, she slipped off her coat and casually draped it over the chair, saying, " *It's so nice to be able to do that without being ashamed of the state of the lining."*

As previously mentioned Imogen was still on good terms with Britten and continued writing a book about him that she had begun in 1953. This was published in 1966 and was remarkable for its anecdotes and insights into the composer's life that only someone who had worked closely with him could aspire to write.

In July of the same year she received the news that she had been made a Fellow of the Royal College of Music.

In 1967 she became involved in various matters concerning the new concert hall at Snape Maltings. The conversion of the old buildings realised a dream that Britten had cherished since 1952. The Queen and Prince Philip, who also attended the opening concert, opened the Hall on 2nd June, the first day of the Festival. The evening was a personal triumph for Imogen as she was able to share the rostrum with Britten to conduct her father's *St. Paul's Suite.* A member of the Aldeburgh Festival Singers recalled the emotion they all felt at this performance. *"Several of us said we would be happy to die there and then!"*

A critic declared, *"It was as if the composer's spirit descended upon her. She lived the music so vividly that it would have been no surprise if she had suddenly risen in a state of levitation."* There was so much applause that Britten had to lead her out a second time, to acknowledge it.

Now, at the age of 60, Imogen decided to retire from conducting the Purcell Singers in order to complete a backlog of editing and writing. In July she accepted an honorary degree from Essex University.

In 1969 she continued her schedule of lectures and recordings until forced to stop for a while, due to the death of her mother, Isobel, at the age of 92. The funeral took place at Ipswich Crematorium in the presence of a small group of mourners. These included Imogen, her mother's daily help, the woman who came in to *sleep,* the Thaxted taxi driver, and Rosamund Strode, who had driven her there.

In 1969, after two successful Festivals in the new venue at the Maltings, the opening night proved a disaster when fire gutted the building. Imogen was immediately involved in rescheduling events at alternative venues.

In July of that year she was honoured with another degree, this time a Doctorate from the University of Exeter. Her celebrity status seemed to be in huge demand. She witnessed the dedication of a Gustav Holst Memorial window at the James Allen's Girls School, attended a "Women of the Year" luncheon, in London, opened new buildings at Saffron Walden College and planted a copper beech tree in her role of President of the Woodbridge Orchestral Society.

The following Spring she was taken into hospital with bronchitis. This left her very weak and in need of a lengthy time to recuperate. She was very grateful when the young composer, Colin Matthews took over some of her work for Britten, and by April she began to perk up and look forward to taking a holiday in the Lake District.

In July she went to the Royal Academy of Music to receive an honorary degree.

By 1972 she had finally finished her decade's work on her father's music and handed it to her publisher. She had effectively retired from conducting, concentrating her efforts on research and editing. With her father's centenary only a year away, Donald Mitchell at Faber raised the idea of producing a complete scholarly edition of his work. As previously mentioned, Imogen, assisted by Colin Matthews, completed this publication which was issued in 1974.

The year of Gustav's centenary was celebrated with a whirlwind of events. Imogen had organised concerts and lectures, negotiated for performances of *Savitri* and *The Wandering Scholar* to be given at Sadlers Wells, and had an exhibition set up of Gustav's life and music at the Aldeburgh Festival and the Royal Festival Hall. Also plans were made to open, to the public, the house in Cheltenham in which he was born.

At last Imogen had the satisfaction of knowing that her father's legacy was now an integral part of the 20th century musical scene in England. Mass media ensured that his music was heard and her editorial work on his behalf was readily available to students and musicians. In recognition of this work Imogen was awarded a CBE in the New Year's Honours List of 1975.

This hectic schedule, at the age of 67, proved very demanding. In the autumn of her father's centenary year, she was taken ill. At first it was thought to be from exhaustion, but when admitted to hospital it appeared that the problem was more serious. She wrote to inform Britten that she would be having her right kidney removed in January and wouldn't be able to resume her normal work until June.

Britten whose health had also been deteriorating over the past years had recently had major heart surgery. The bond between them seemed to develop a new closeness, due to their ill health, and they found comfort in sharing reminiscences about their past.

Imogen's health greatly improved after her operation but sadly Britten's did not. He died on 4th December 1976 and was buried in the churchyard at Aldeburgh three days later.

In 1978 she was delighted to discover that she was a beneficiary in his will. Having always lived a frugal life she decided to spend the money on assisting several intelligent children between the ages of 10 and 13.

With Pears she attended a memorial concert for Britten, at Dartington, then returned to Aldeburgh to dedicate her time to her father's music that involved working with Colin Matthews on the Collected Facsimile Edition.

In 1977 she had finally stepped down from her position as Artistic Director of the Festival and in 1978 she was able to attend as a member of the public.

On April 28th 1979 the Queen Mother opened the new buildings of the Britten-Pears school, at Snape. Imogen had the honour of showing her around the Gustav Holst library stocked with music and books that she had donated.

She was glad to shed the responsibility of her father's legacy to others especially Colin Matthews who had become Managing Director of G & I Holst Ltd.

At the age of 70 Imogen found that she no longer needed to hurry. *"There are advantages in walking at an "Andante piacevole" speed, for it leaves time to look at the changing colours of a sunset."* She could also linger at the breakfast table, listening to her favourite Haydn Quartet.

She enjoyed the benefits of being retired, of having time to learn a Shakespeare sonnet or take up another activity such as studying Russian grammar.

She was also glad not to have to buy new clothes preferring to be able to extend wearing some of her old favourites. *"I'm still wearing the wool-embroidered evening jacket I bought for £5.00 in South Kensington in 1928 on my way to a lesson at the Royal College of Music."*

In this Autumn period of her life Colin Matthews later wrote,
"How can one begin to describe Imogen Holst?

Her voice - measured, modulated and careful, beautifully enunciated, a surprisingly deep laugh ---- with a short, sharp and quintessential "ha!" of amusement.

Colours – soft yellow ochres, browns and olive greens predominated in her clothing ---- she did not like bright colours and had a loathing of a particular shade of purple.

Noise – the roar of a London street could cause her physical pain."

In 1980 Imogen emerged from her retirement, temporarily,

to help arrange a gala concert to celebrate Peter Pears' 70th birthday. She put together a piece entitled *A greeting*, from the music of several composers including Bach and Britten. This was performed on June 20th 1980.

With her creativity stimulated, over the next four years she began her "Autumn" of compositions, pieces written for friends, a piano duet written for William Servaes, who retired, at Christmas, from his position as General Manager of the Aldeburgh Festival, and also *Song for a well-loved Librarian* for Fred Ferry, the first librarian of the Britten-Pears Library. This was followed by the *String Quintet* of 1982 published by Faber in recognition of her 75th birthday. It was on seeing the proofs of the printed score that she acknowledged to friends, *"I feel like a real composer."*

In 1983 her health became a concern. Over the past few years she had suffered from angina. It was at this time that she decided to pass on her Holst manuscripts to the Holst Foundation and all her Britten material to the Britten-Pears library.

However she still planned ahead as a composer, accepting four commissions in 1984. One was *Homage to William Morris* for the William Morris Society to commemorate the 150th anniversary of his birth. Unfortunately she did not live to hear its first performance, which took place on March 24th, shortly after her death.

She also wrote a sextet for recorders for the Guildford Society of Recorder Players and a *Recorder Concerto* for the 1984 Cricklade Festival.

She became involved in a new revision of *The Music of Gustav Holst*, for Oxford University Press for which she was asked to contribute some new chapters.

However her health began to deteriorate rapidly. She tired very quickly and died, from a heart attack, in her bed on 9th March 1984. She had telephoned her secretary, Helen Lilley, that morning, asking her to go round, and also the doctor, who, immediately left to arrange for her to be taken into hospital. However this never happened. Helen Lilley recalled,

" She said that she was thirsty so I fetched some water and

stayed by the bed to help with the cup. She smiled and thanked me in the usual Imo way. Everything was still. Her head drooped gently sideways and I felt she had slipped away, absolutely peacefully, and without fuss. I was so glad that she had not been alone."

Her funeral took place on 14th March. She was buried in the churchyard of St. Peter and St. Paul, Aldeburgh near to Benjamin Britten. Peter Pears read a passage from her father's translation of *The Hymn of Jesus* and the final chorale from Bach's *St. John's Passion* was played as the mourners left.

There is no doubt that Imogen lived her life through music. She had inherited her talent from her father, who openly encouraged her and was able to follow her interests in a very productive way thus contributing greatly to British musical life in the 20th century. She composed a surprisingly large amount of music much of which was written on commission, but about thirty works were written, in a sudden burst of creativity during the last twenty years of her life.

The programme for the 1984 Aldeburgh Festival included a two-page selection of tributes that had been received by her colleagues, and John Thomson wrote an obituary in the journal Early Music.

"Her presence will always be felt in Aldeburgh Parish Church," he wrote. *"IH would appear, stride to the rostrum purposefully, quickly acknowledge applause, and turn to the matter in hand, to bring iridescently to life facets of that tradition to which her own life had been dedicated."*

Selective list of works

Stage
Meddling in Magic (ballet) 1930
Love in a Mist or *The Blue Haired Stranger* (ballet) 1935. Music now lost.
Young Beichan (puppet opera) 1945.
Benedict and Beatrice (opera)1950

Other Works.
Orchestral.
Suite for small orchestra, 1927.
Persephone (Overture), 1929
Concerto for String Orchestra, 1935.
Suite for String orchestra 1943.
Variations on "Loth to depart" for String orchestra, 1963.
Trianon Suite, 1965.
Woodbridge Suite,1969.
Joyce's Divertimento,1976.
Deben Calendar, 1977.

Chamber
Quintet for oboe and strings, 1928.
String Quartet "Phantasy", 1928.
Sonata for violin and 'cello, 1930.
String Trio, 1944.
Two String Quartets.
No.1 1946.
No. 2.1950.
String Trio, 1962.
Fall of the Leaf for 'cello, 1963.
Duo for viola and piano, 1968.
String Quintet, 1982.

Vocal
A Hymne to Christ for SATB, 1940.

4 Songs for soprano and piano,1944.
5 Songs for sopranos and altos, 1944.

Lavabo inter Innocentes, for sopranos and altos,1955.
The Sun's Journey, cantata for soprano and alto and small orchestra, 1965.
Hallo my Fancy, counter tenor, tenor, sopranos and bass, 1972.
Homage to William Morris, bass and double bass, 1984.

Works for brass bands, wind bands, recorder groups, chorus and orchestra and chamber groups.
Publisher's used : - Boosey & Hawkes, Cramer, Faber, Novello, OUPress.

Bibliography

ABRAHAM, Gerald. *Rimsky-Korsakov, A Short Biography*
Duckworth, London. (1945)

BLAUKOPF, Kurt and Herta, *Mahler, His Life, Work and World*
Thames and Hudson, London (1991)

COLERIDGE-TAYLOR, Avril, *The Heritage of Samuel Coleridge-Taylor*
Dennis Dobson, London (1979)

GLOVER, Jane. *Mozart's Women.*
Harper Perennial, New York. U.S.A (2007)

HENSEL, Sebastian. *The Mendelssohn Family (1729-1847)* 2nd revised edition
First Published - Harper and Brothers, New York (1882)

HOLST, Imogen. *Gustav Holst. A Biography*
Faber and Faber. London.(2008)

GIROUD, Françoise. *Alma Mahler or the Art of Being Loved.*
Oxford University Press (1991)

GROGAN, Christopher, with Rosamund Strode and Christopher Tinker.
Imogen Holst, A Life in Music.
The Boydell Press. England. (2007)

KUPFERBERG. Herbert. *Felix Mendelssohn. His Life, his Family, his Music.*
Charles Scribner's Sons. New York. U.S.A (1972)

LAURENCE, Anya. *Women of Notes.*
Bib/2
Richard Rosen Press, Inc. New York, U.S.A (1978)

REICH, Nancy B. *Clara Schumann, The Artist and the Woman.*
Oxford University Press. (1989)

RESPIGHI, Elsa. *Fifty Years of a Life in Music 1905-1955*
The Edwin Mellen Press. U.S.A

RIMSKY-KORSAKOV. *My Musical Life*
Faber and Faber, London/Boston (1989)
Edited by SADIE, Julie Anne & SAMUEL, Rhian.

THE NORTON/GROVE DICTIONARY OF WOMEN COMPOSERS
Macmillan Press. London. (1995)

STEEGMANN, Monica, *Clara Schumann.*
Haus Publishing. London. (2004)

TILLARD, Françoise. *Fanny Mendelssohn*
Amadeus Press, Oregon U.S.A (1992)

Lightning Source UK Ltd.
Milton Keynes UK
UKOW010642121011

180158UK00001B/36/P

9 780755 213443